Louise Brooks:
DETECTIVE

ISBN: 978-1-56163-952-6
Library of Congress Control Number: 2015902716
© 2015 Rick Geary
Printed in China

1st printing June 2015

Comicslit is an imprint
and trademark of

NANTIER · BEALL · MINOUSTCHINE
Publishing inc.
new york

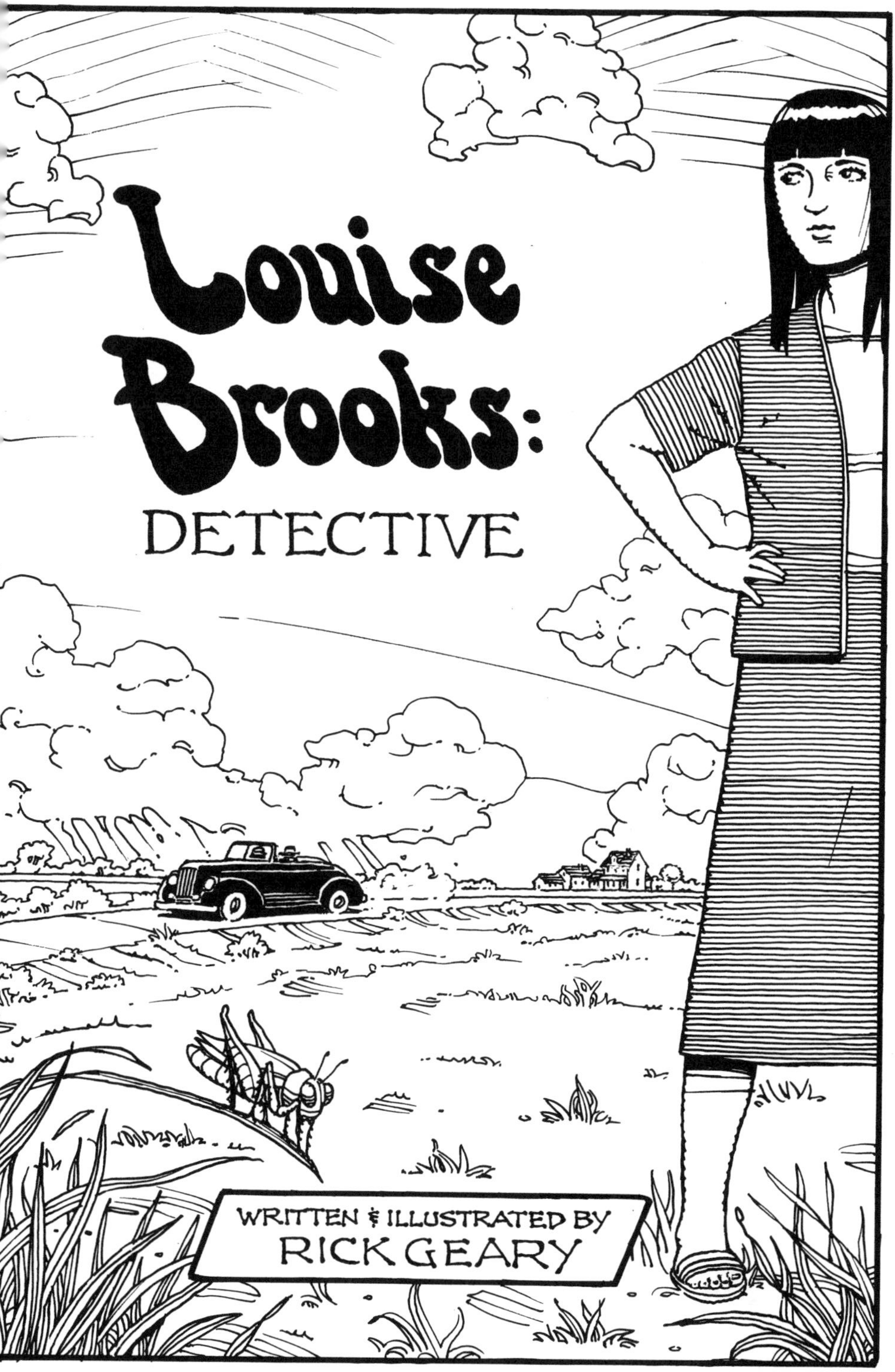

Louise Brooks:
DETECTIVE
WRITTEN & ILLUSTRATED BY
RICK GEARY

Also available by Geary:
A Treasury of Victorian Murder:
Vol. 1, pb.: $9.95, E-book: $6.99
Jack The Ripper pb.: $9.95, E-book: $6.99
The Borden Tragedy, pb.: $9.99
The Fatal Bullet, pb.: $9.95, E-book: $6.99
The Mystery of Mary Rogers
hc.: $15.95, E-book: $6.99
The Beast of Chicago, E-book: $6.99
The Murder of Abraham Lincoln
pb.: $9.95, hc.: $15.95, E-book: $6.99
The Bloody Benders, pb.: $9.95, E-book: $6.99
The Case of Madeleine Smith
pb.: $8.95, hc.: $15.95
A Treasury of XXth Century Murder:
The Lindbergh Child
pb.: $9.95, hc.: $15.95, E-book: $6.99
Famous Players
pb.: $9.95, hc.: $15.95, , E-book: $6.99
The Axe-Man of New Orleans
hc.: $15.99, E-book: $6.99
The Lives of Sacco & Vanzetti
hc.: $15.99, E-book: $6.99
Lovers Lane
hc.: $15.99, E-book: $6.99
Madison Square Tragedy
hc.: $15.99, E-book: $6.99
A Treasury of Victorian Murder Compendium
hc.: $24.99
A Treasury of Victorian Murder Compendium II
hc.: $29.99

A Treasury of Victorian Murder
Jack the Ripper
A TREASURY OF VICTORIAN MURDER
The Borden Tragedy
Rick Geary
The Mystery of Mary Rogers
The Beast of Chicago
THE MURDER OF ABRAHAM LINCOLN
The Case of Madeleine Smith
The Saga of the Bloody Benders
RICK GEARY
LINDBERGH CHILD
FAMOUS PLAYERS
THE TERRIBLE AXE-MAN OF NEW ORLEANS
THE LIVES OF SACCO & VANZETTI
LOVERS' LANE
MADISON SQUARE TRAGEDY
THE MURDER OF STANFORD WHITE
A TREASURY OF VICTORIAN MURDER COMPENDIUM
A TREASURY OF VICTORIAN MURDER COMPENDIUM II

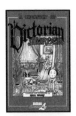

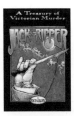

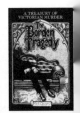

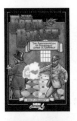

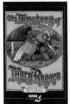

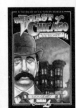

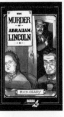

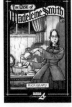

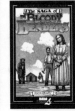

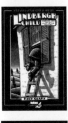

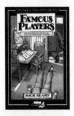

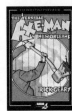

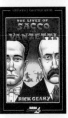

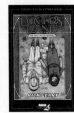

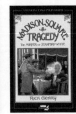

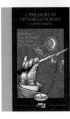

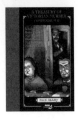

LOUISE
An Introduction

"There is no Garbo, there is no Dietrich, there is only Louise Brooks."
Henri Langlois, *Cinematheque Francaise.*

Though her name is largely forgotten today, the image of Louise Brooks remains among the most iconic of the twentieth century.

She was born in 1906 in the town of Cherryvale, Kansas, and grew up in the nearby city of Wichita.

A professional dancer from age 16, she toured the country with the Ruth St. Denis troupe, and performed in New York with the Ziegfeld Follies and George White's Scandals. She was hired by Paramount Pictures and made several films at their Long Island studio before moving to Hollywood in 1927.

She became an increasingly recognizable presence in several features and was on the brink of major stardom when, in 1928, she declined to renew her Paramount contract. She travelled to Germany to work with the director G.W. Pabst in the film Pandora's Box, which has since become a landmark in screen eroticism.

She stayed in Europe to make two more films and returned to Hollywood in 1930. But her career had lost its momentum, and she languished in small parts in undistinguished pictures. For two years, she danced in a nightblub act, but by 1940, at age 33, she began to see her prospects dimming. By then, having been married and divorced twice, her view of human relationships was decidedly sour. So, with no income and nowhere else to go, she made a "strategic retreat" —to her parents' home in Wichita, Kansas.

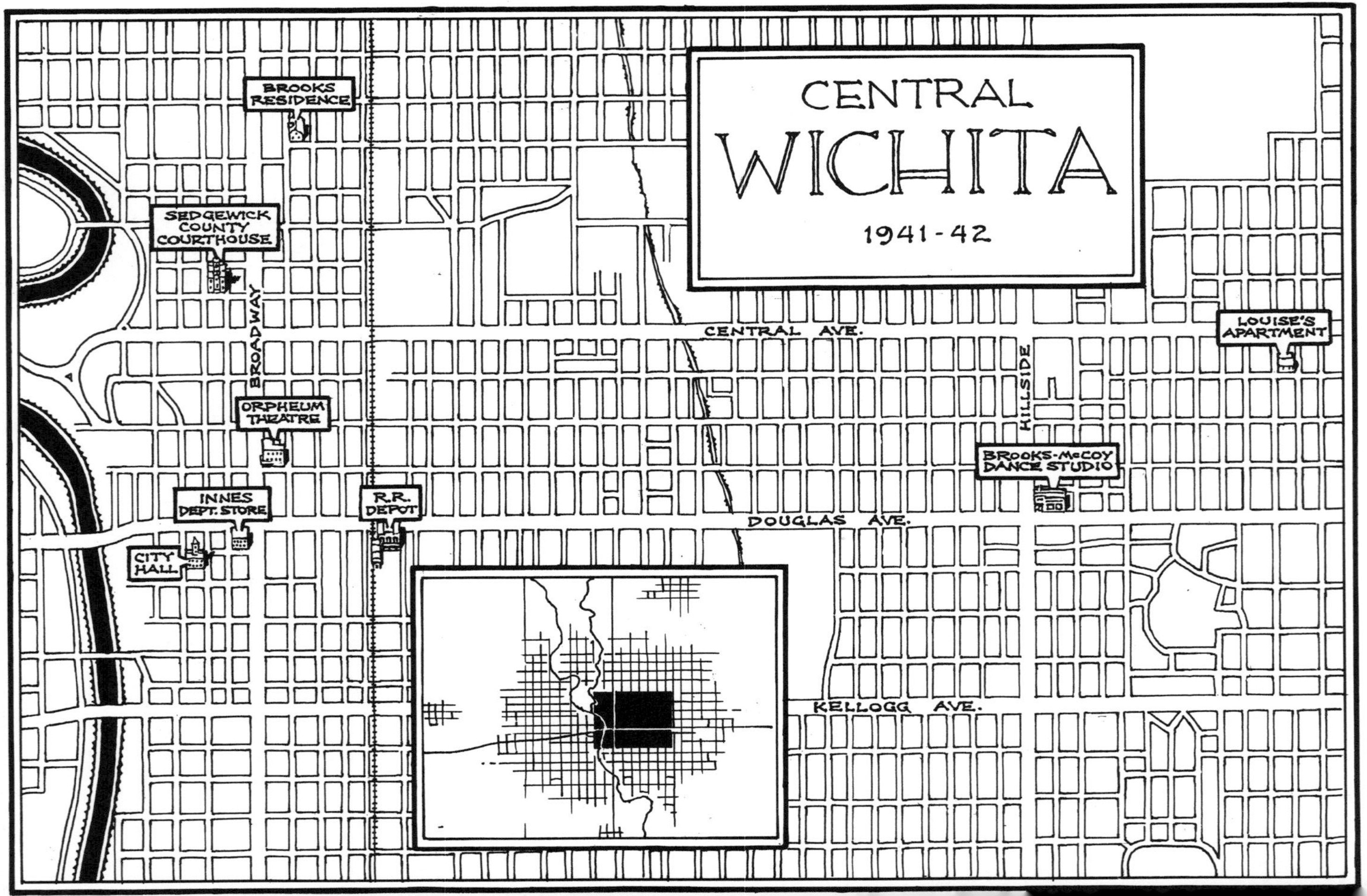
CENTRAL
WICHITA
1941-42
BROOKS RESIDENCE
SEDGEWICK COUNTY COURTHOUSE
BROADWAY
ORPHEUM THEATRE
INNES DEPT. STORE
CITY HALL
R.R. DEPOT
CENTRAL AVE.
DOUGLAS AVE.
KELLOGG AVE.
HILLSIDE
BROOKS-McCOY DANCE STUDIO
LOUISE'S APARTMENT

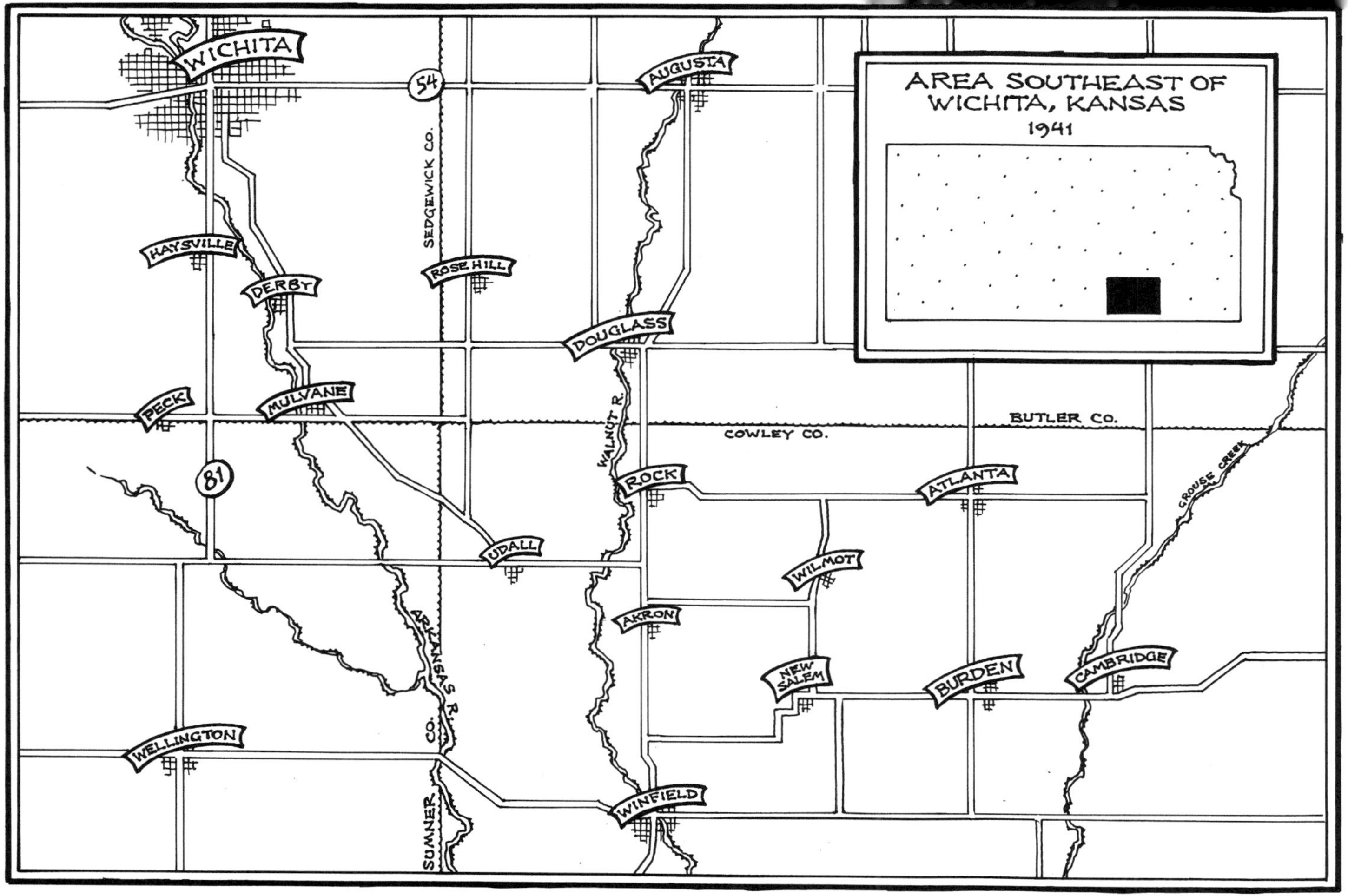
AREA SOUTHEAST OF
WICHITA, KANSAS
1941
WICHITA
54
AUGUSTA
SEDGEWICK CO.
HAYSVILLE
DERBY
ROSE HILL
DOUGLASS
PECK
MULVANE
BUTLER CO.
COWLEY CO.
WALNUT R.
81
ROCK
ATLANTA
GROUSE CREEK
UDALL
WILMOT
ARKANSAS R.
AKRON
NEW SALEM
BURDEN
CAMBRIDGE
WELLINGTON
SUMNER CO.
WINFIELD

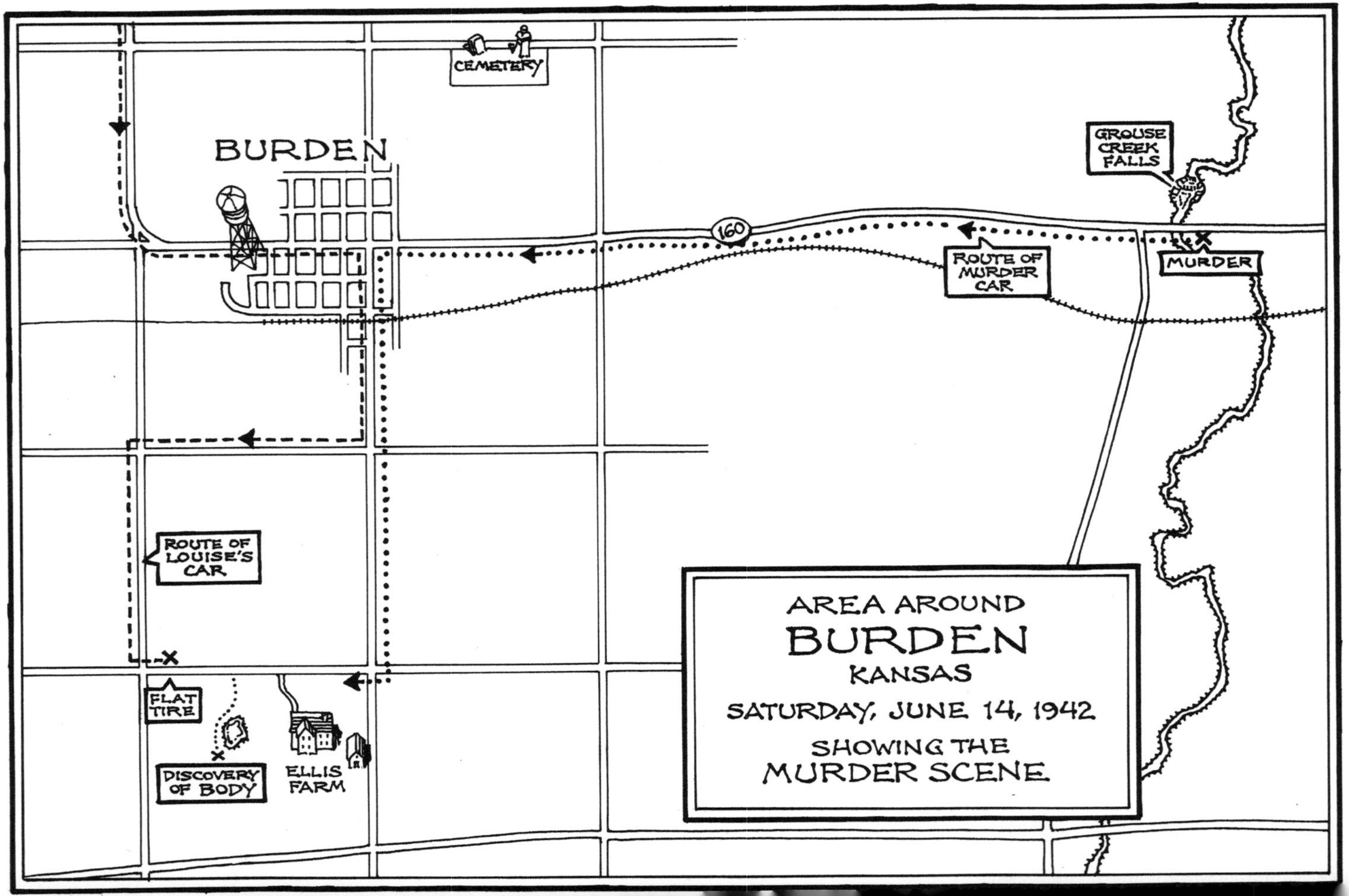
AREA AROUND
BURDEN
KANSAS
SATURDAY, JUNE 14, 1942
SHOWING THE
MURDER SCENE
BURDEN
CEMETERY
GROUSE CREEK FALLS
160
MURDER
ROUTE OF MURDER CAR
ROUTE OF LOUISE'S CAR
FLAT TIRE
DISCOVERY OF BODY
ELLIS FARM

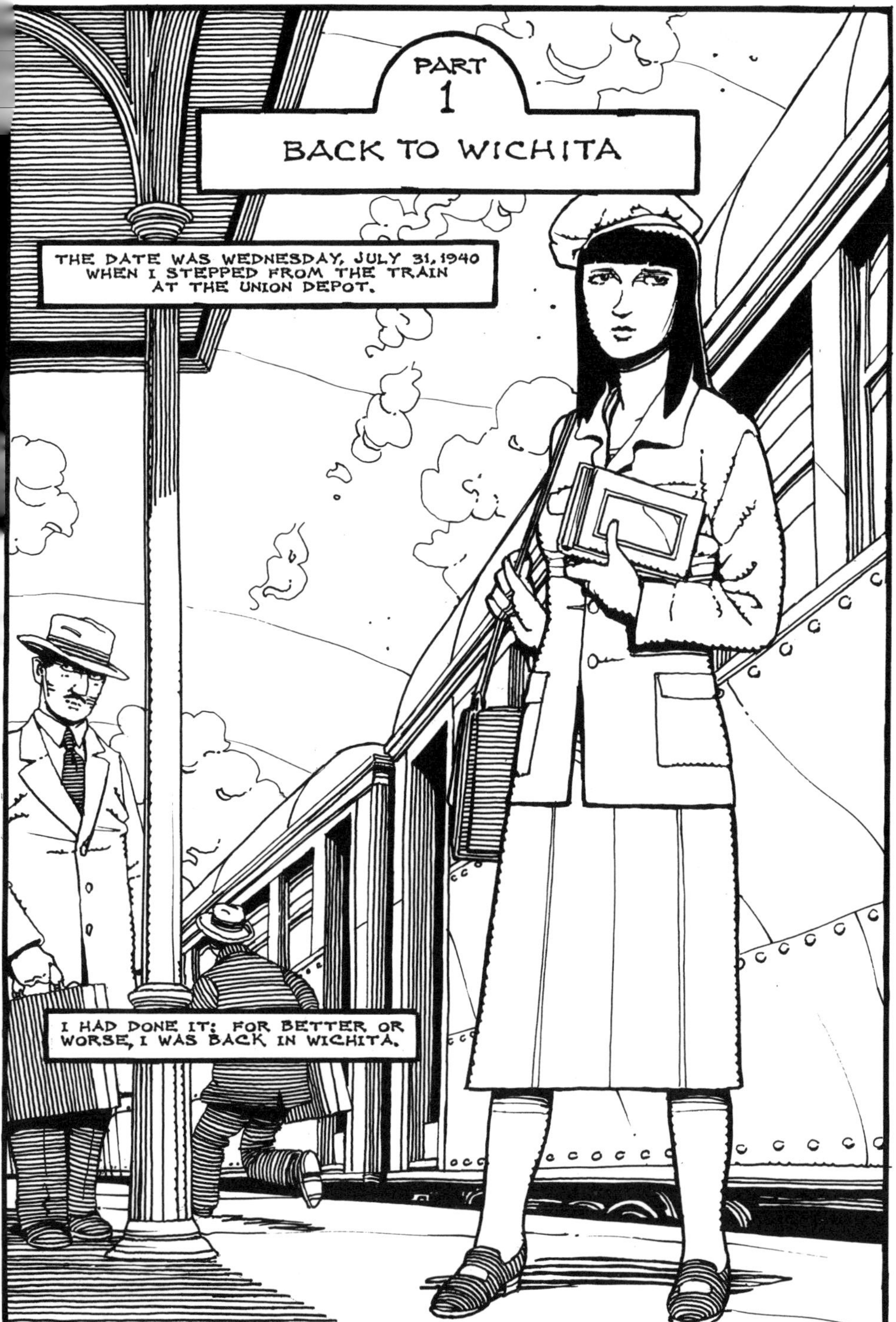
PART
1
BACK TO WICHITA
THE DATE WAS WEDNESDAY, JULY 31, 1940 WHEN I STEPPED FROM THE TRAIN AT THE UNION DEPOT.
I HAD DONE IT: FOR BETTER OR WORSE, I WAS BACK IN WICHITA.

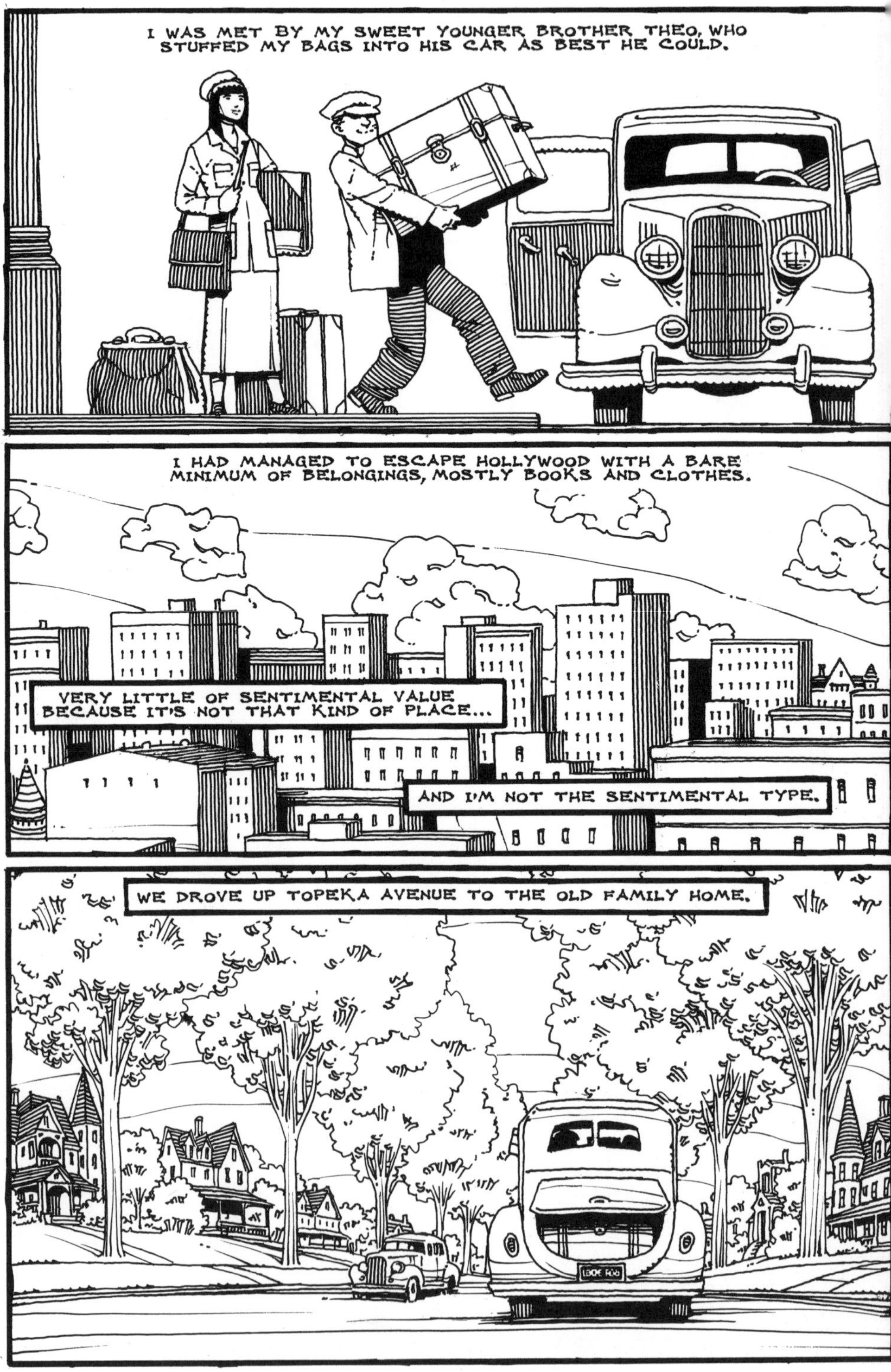
I WAS MET BY MY SWEET YOUNGER BROTHER THEO, WHO STUFFED MY BAGS INTO HIS CAR AS BEST HE COULD.
I HAD MANAGED TO ESCAPE HOLLYWOOD WITH A BARE MINIMUM OF BELONGINGS, MOSTLY BOOKS AND CLOTHES.
VERY LITTLE OF SENTIMENTAL VALUE BECAUSE IT'S NOT THAT KIND OF PLACE...
AND I'M NOT THE SENTIMENTAL TYPE.
WE DROVE UP TOPEKA AVENUE TO THE OLD FAMILY HOME.

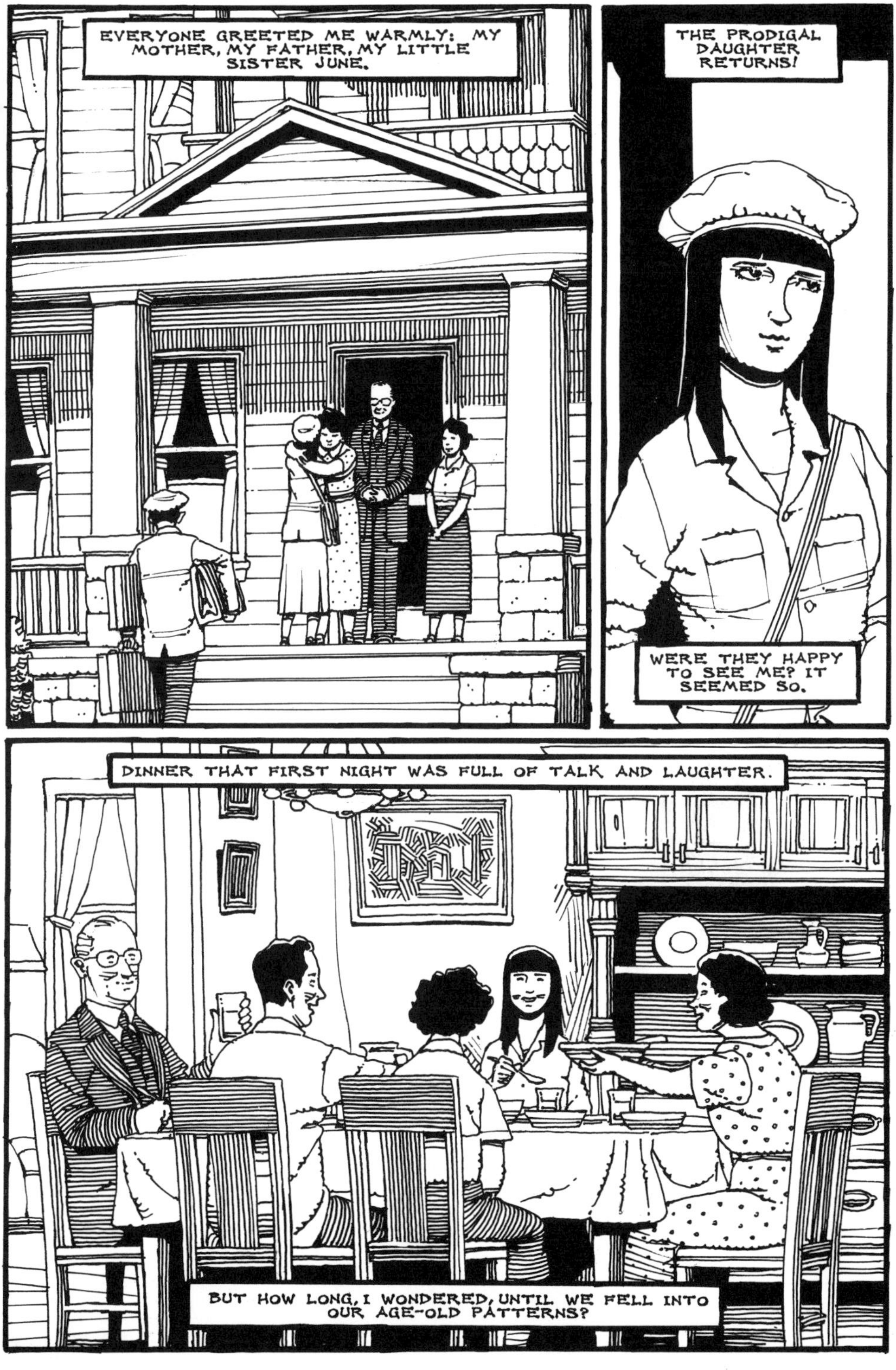
EVERYONE GREETED ME WARMLY: MY MOTHER, MY FATHER, MY LITTLE SISTER JUNE.
THE PRODIGAL DAUGHTER RETURNS!
WERE THEY HAPPY TO SEE ME? IT SEEMED SO.
DINNER THAT FIRST NIGHT WAS FULL OF TALK AND LAUGHTER.
BUT HOW LONG, I WONDERED, UNTIL WE FELL INTO OUR AGE-OLD PATTERNS?

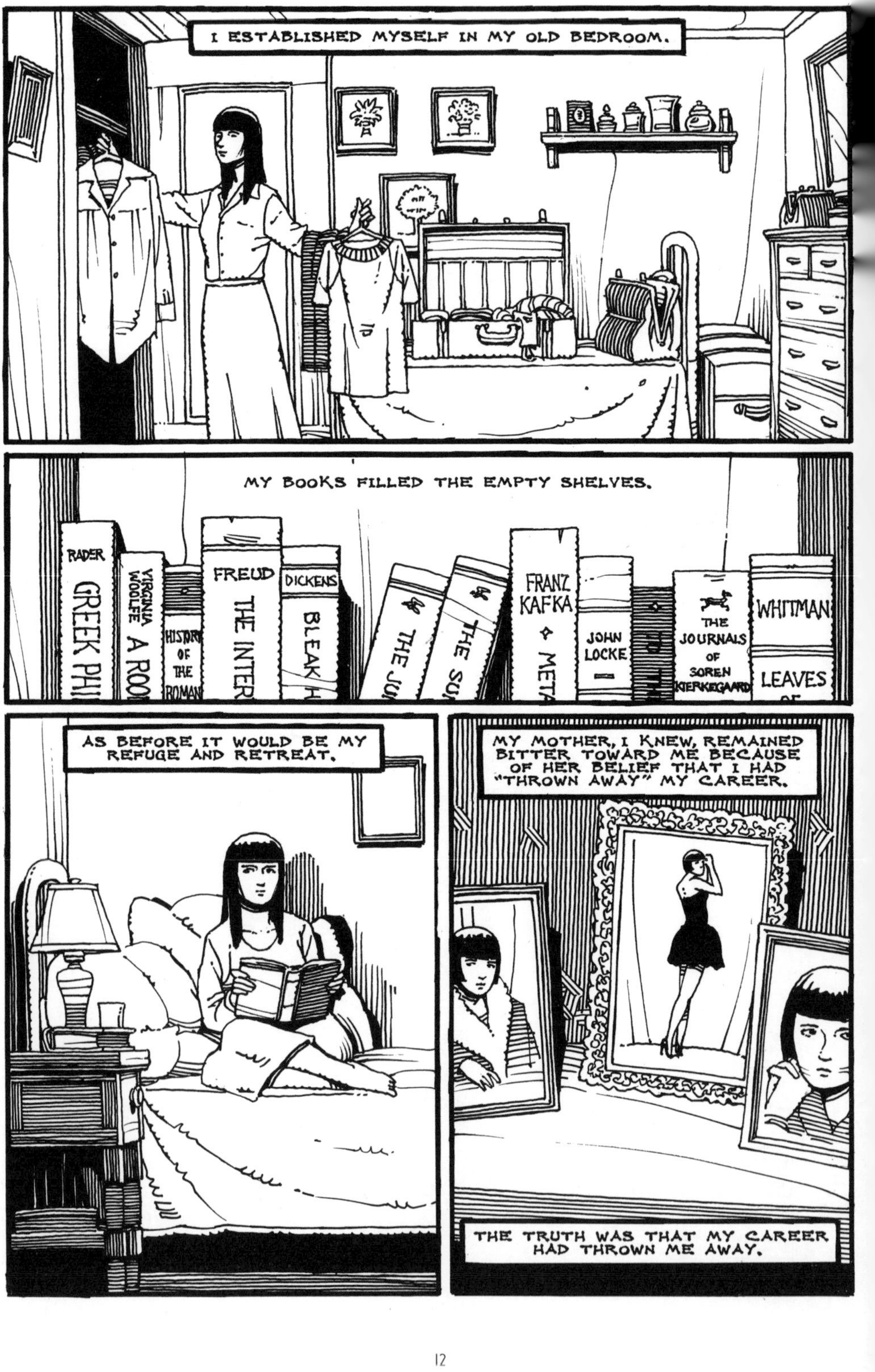
I ESTABLISHED MYSELF IN MY OLD BEDROOM.
MY BOOKS FILLED THE EMPTY SHELVES.
RADER
VIRGINIA WOOLFE
FREUD
DICKENS
FRANZ KAFKA
JOHN LOCKE
THE JOURNALS OF SOREN KIERKEGAARD
WHITMAN
LEAVES
AS BEFORE IT WOULD BE MY REFUGE AND RETREAT.
MY MOTHER, I KNEW, REMAINED BITTER TOWARD ME BECAUSE OF HER BELIEF THAT I HAD "THROWN AWAY" MY CAREER.
THE TRUTH WAS THAT MY CAREER HAD THROWN ME AWAY.

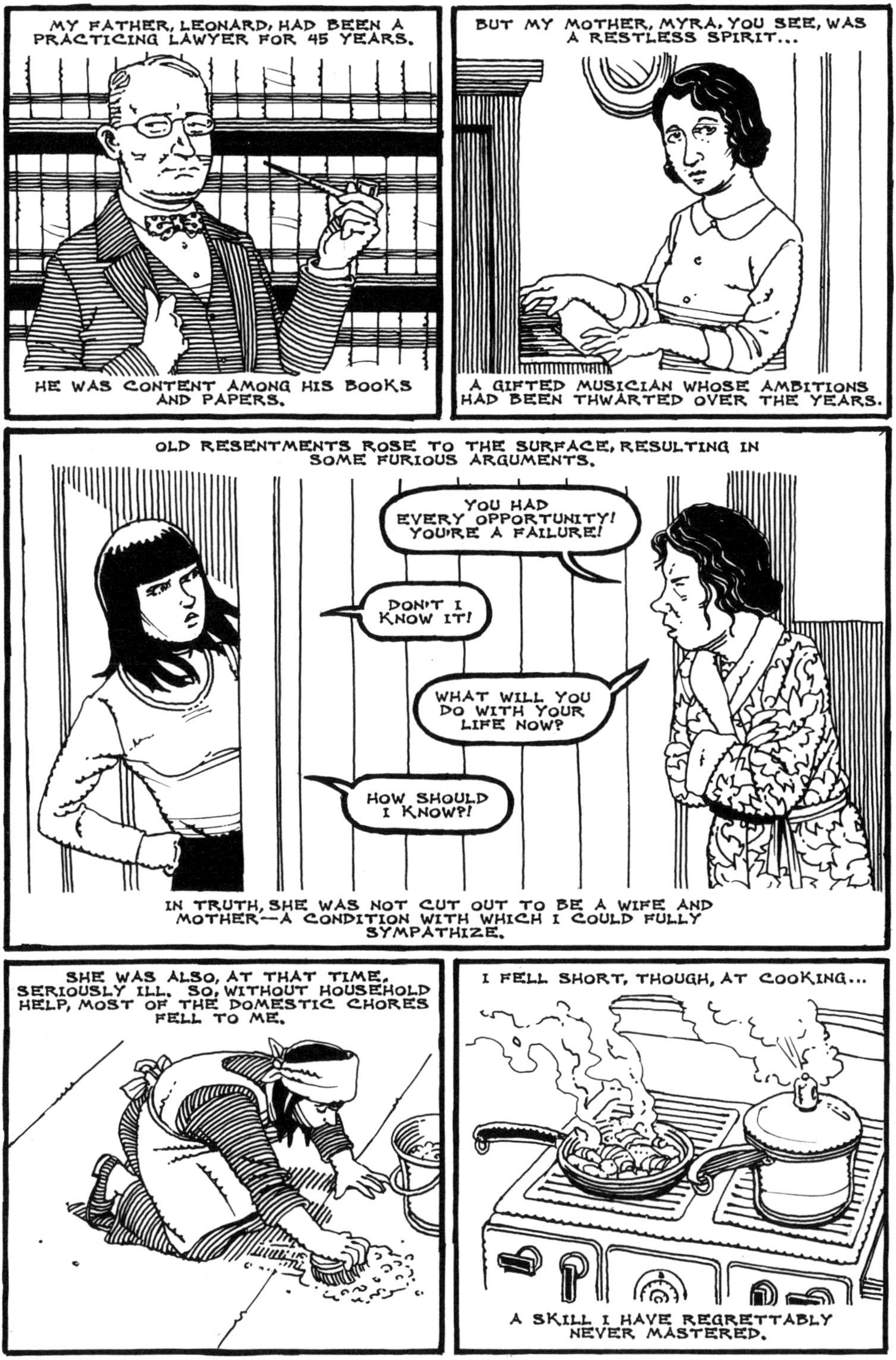
MY FATHER, LEONARD, HAD BEEN A PRACTICING LAWYER FOR 45 YEARS.
HE WAS CONTENT AMONG HIS BOOKS AND PAPERS.
BUT MY MOTHER, MYRA, YOU SEE, WAS A RESTLESS SPIRIT...
A GIFTED MUSICIAN WHOSE AMBITIONS HAD BEEN THWARTED OVER THE YEARS.
OLD RESENTMENTS ROSE TO THE SURFACE, RESULTING IN SOME FURIOUS ARGUMENTS.
YOU HAD EVERY OPPORTUNITY! YOU'RE A FAILURE!
DON'T I KNOW IT!
WHAT WILL YOU DO WITH YOUR LIFE NOW?
HOW SHOULD I KNOW?!
IN TRUTH, SHE WAS NOT CUT OUT TO BE A WIFE AND MOTHER—A CONDITION WITH WHICH I COULD FULLY SYMPATHIZE.
SHE WAS ALSO, AT THAT TIME, SERIOUSLY ILL. SO, WITHOUT HOUSEHOLD HELP, MOST OF THE DOMESTIC CHORES FELL TO ME.
I FELL SHORT, THOUGH, AT COOKING...
A SKILL I HAVE REGRETTABLY NEVER MASTERED.

IN THE EVENINGS WE LISTENED TO
THE RADIO.

AND I WAS MUCH ENTERTAINED
BY THE LOCAL NEWSPAPERS,
THE EAGLE AND THE BEACON...

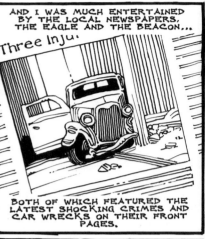

Three Inju

BOTH OF WHICH FEATURED THE
LATEST SHOCKING CRIMES AND
CAR WRECKS ON THEIR FRONT
PAGES.

THE CITY, AT THAT TIME,
WAS TRANSFIXED BY A
SENSATIONAL MURDER CASE.

RDER
SIDE

A WEALTHY WIDOW NAMED
EDNA LEACH HAD BEEN
STABBED TO DEATH IN
THE BEDROOM OF HER
HOME IN EAST WICHITA.

IT HAD ALL THE MAKINGS OF A GENUINE LOCKED-
ROOM MYSTERY.

NEW
FOUN

No Si
in L

THE BEDROOM DOOR WAS LOCKED, AS WAS EVERY
DOOR INTO THE HOUSE, AS PER THE STRICT
REQUIREMENTS OF THE SECURITY-MINDED
VICTIM.

SHE APPARENTLY NEVER GAVE HER
KEYS TO ANYONE NOT EVEN THE
HOUSEKEEPER...

WHO HAD PUT MRS. LEACH TO BED AT
AT 8PM ONE NIGHT AND BECAME
CONCERNED THE NEXT MORNING WHEN
THERE WAS NO RESPONSE TO HER
REPEATED KNOCKING.

AT LAST SHE SUMMONED THE
GARDENER.

HE BROKE THE LOCK ON THE BACK
DOOR AND THEN BURST THROUGH THE
DOOR OF THE LADY'S BEDROOM.

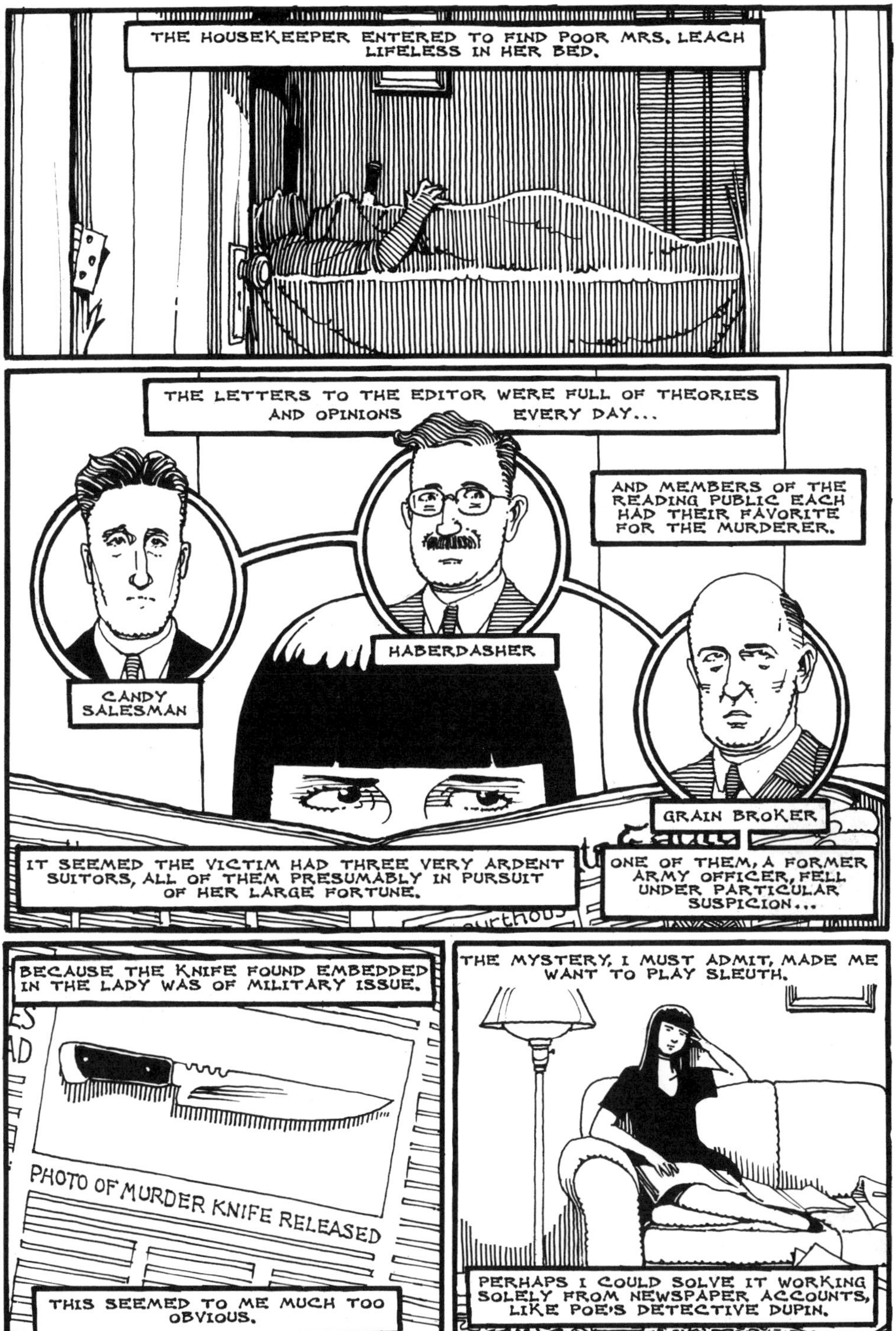
THE HOUSEKEEPER ENTERED TO FIND POOR MRS. LEACH LIFELESS IN HER BED.
THE LETTERS TO THE EDITOR WERE FULL OF THEORIES AND OPINIONS EVERY DAY...
AND MEMBERS OF THE READING PUBLIC EACH HAD THEIR FAVORITE FOR THE MURDERER.
CANDY SALESMAN
HABERDASHER
GRAIN BROKER
IT SEEMED THE VICTIM HAD THREE VERY ARDENT SUITORS, ALL OF THEM PRESUMABLY IN PURSUIT OF HER LARGE FORTUNE.
ONE OF THEM, A FORMER ARMY OFFICER, FELL UNDER PARTICULAR SUSPICION...
BECAUSE THE KNIFE FOUND EMBEDDED IN THE LADY WAS OF MILITARY ISSUE.
PHOTO OF MURDER KNIFE RELEASED
THIS SEEMED TO ME MUCH TOO OBVIOUS.
THE MYSTERY, I MUST ADMIT, MADE ME WANT TO PLAY SLEUTH.
PERHAPS I COULD SOLVE IT WORKING SOLELY FROM NEWSPAPER ACCOUNTS, LIKE POE'S DETECTIVE DUPIN.

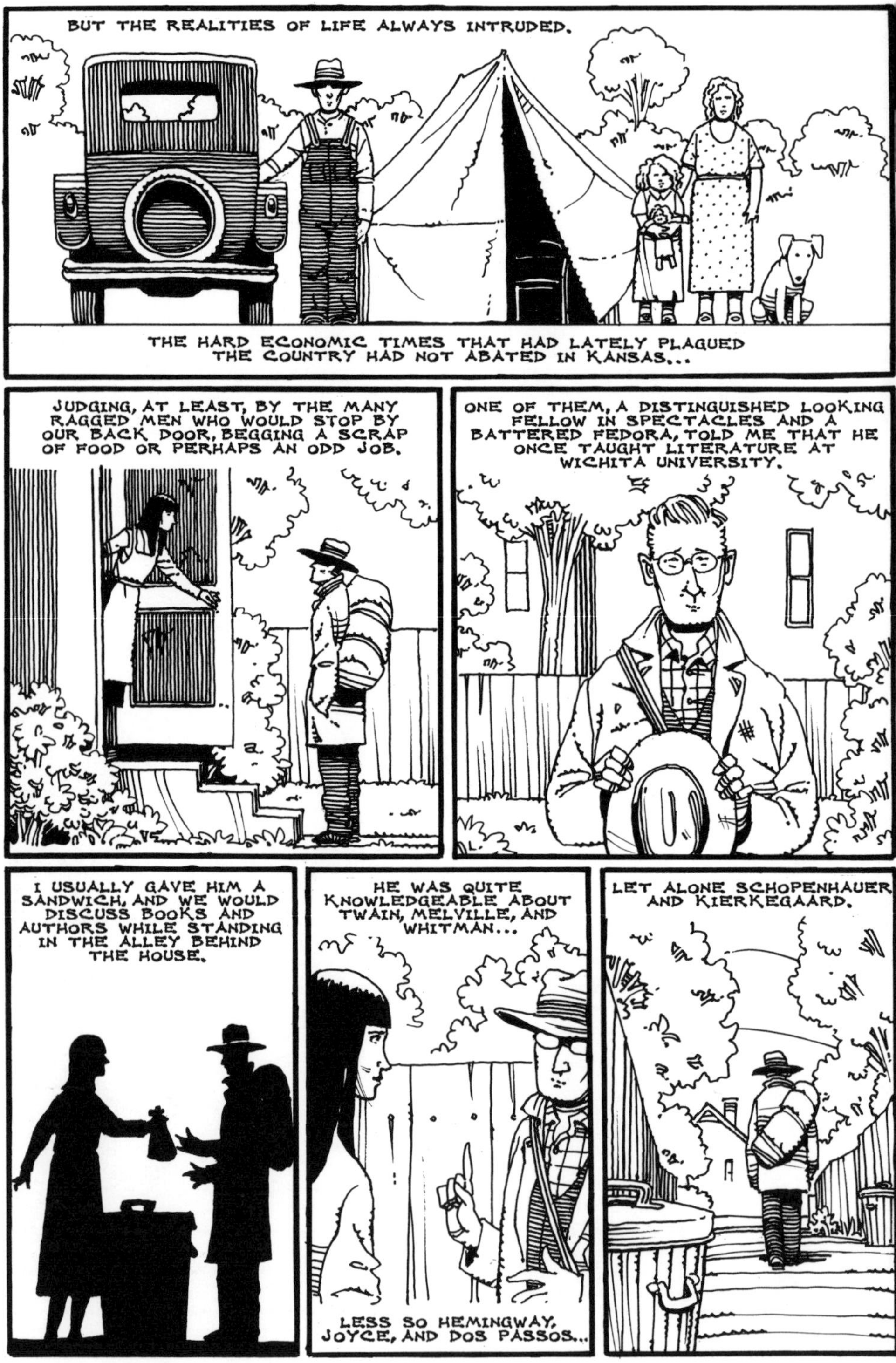
BUT THE REALITIES OF LIFE ALWAYS INTRUDED.
THE HARD ECONOMIC TIMES THAT HAD LATELY PLAGUED THE COUNTRY HAD NOT ABATED IN KANSAS...
JUDGING, AT LEAST, BY THE MANY RAGGED MEN WHO WOULD STOP BY OUR BACK DOOR, BEGGING A SCRAP OF FOOD OR PERHAPS AN ODD JOB.
ONE OF THEM, A DISTINGUISHED LOOKING FELLOW IN SPECTACLES AND A BATTERED FEDORA, TOLD ME THAT HE ONCE TAUGHT LITERATURE AT WICHITA UNIVERSITY.
I USUALLY GAVE HIM A SANDWICH, AND WE WOULD DISCUSS BOOKS AND AUTHORS WHILE STANDING IN THE ALLEY BEHIND THE HOUSE.
HE WAS QUITE KNOWLEDGEABLE ABOUT TWAIN, MELVILLE, AND WHITMAN...
LESS SO HEMINGWAY, JOYCE, AND DOS PASSOS...
LET ALONE SCHOPENHAUER AND KIERKEGAARD.

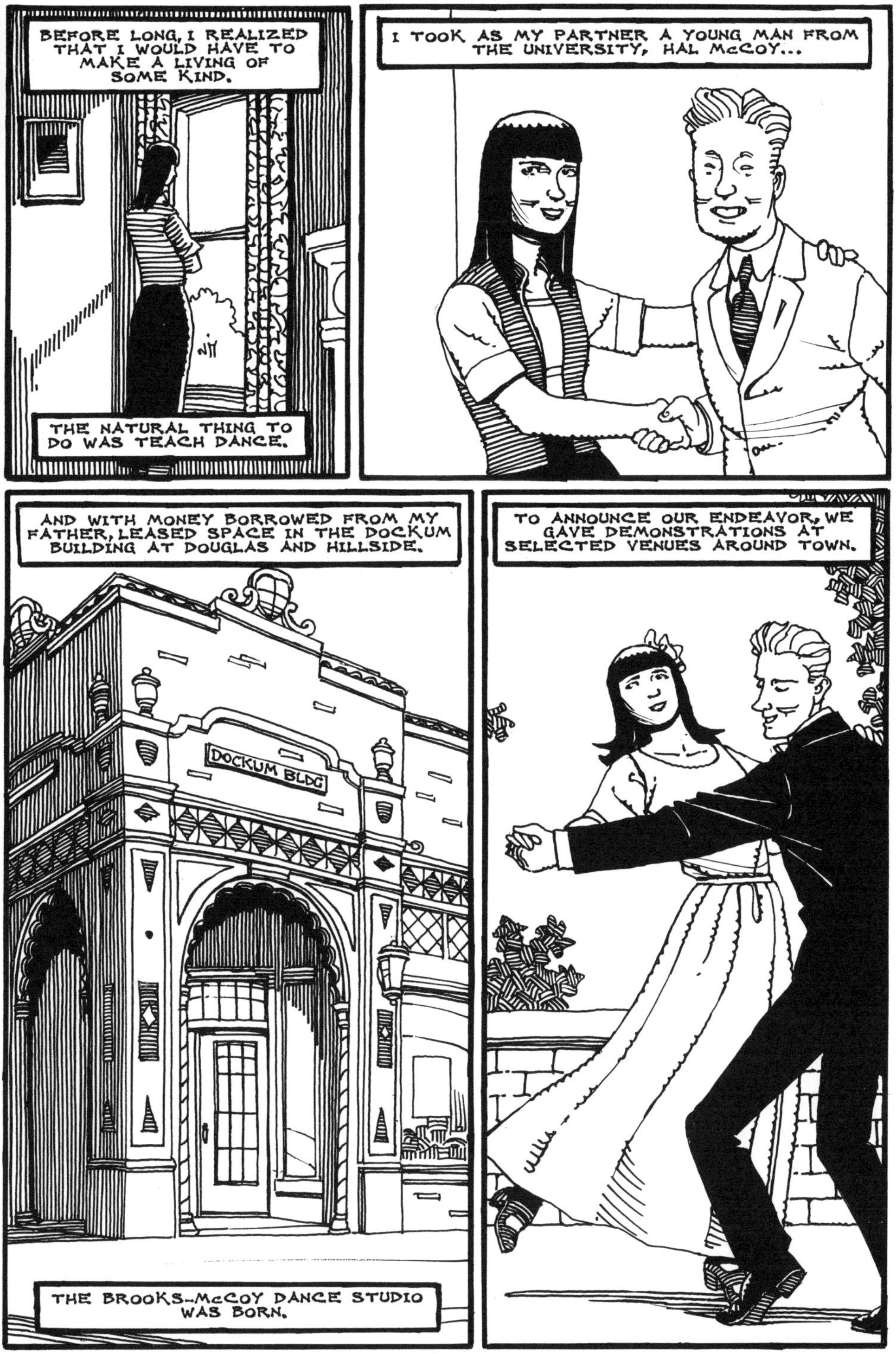
BEFORE LONG, I REALIZED THAT I WOULD HAVE TO MAKE A LIVING OF SOME KIND.
THE NATURAL THING TO DO WAS TEACH DANCE.
I TOOK AS MY PARTNER A YOUNG MAN FROM THE UNIVERSITY, HAL McCOY...
AND WITH MONEY BORROWED FROM MY FATHER, LEASED SPACE IN THE DOCKUM BUILDING AT DOUGLAS AND HILLSIDE.
DOCKUM BLDG
THE BROOKS-McCOY DANCE STUDIO WAS BORN.
TO ANNOUNCE OUR ENDEAVOR, WE GAVE DEMONSTRATIONS AT SELECTED VENUES AROUND TOWN.

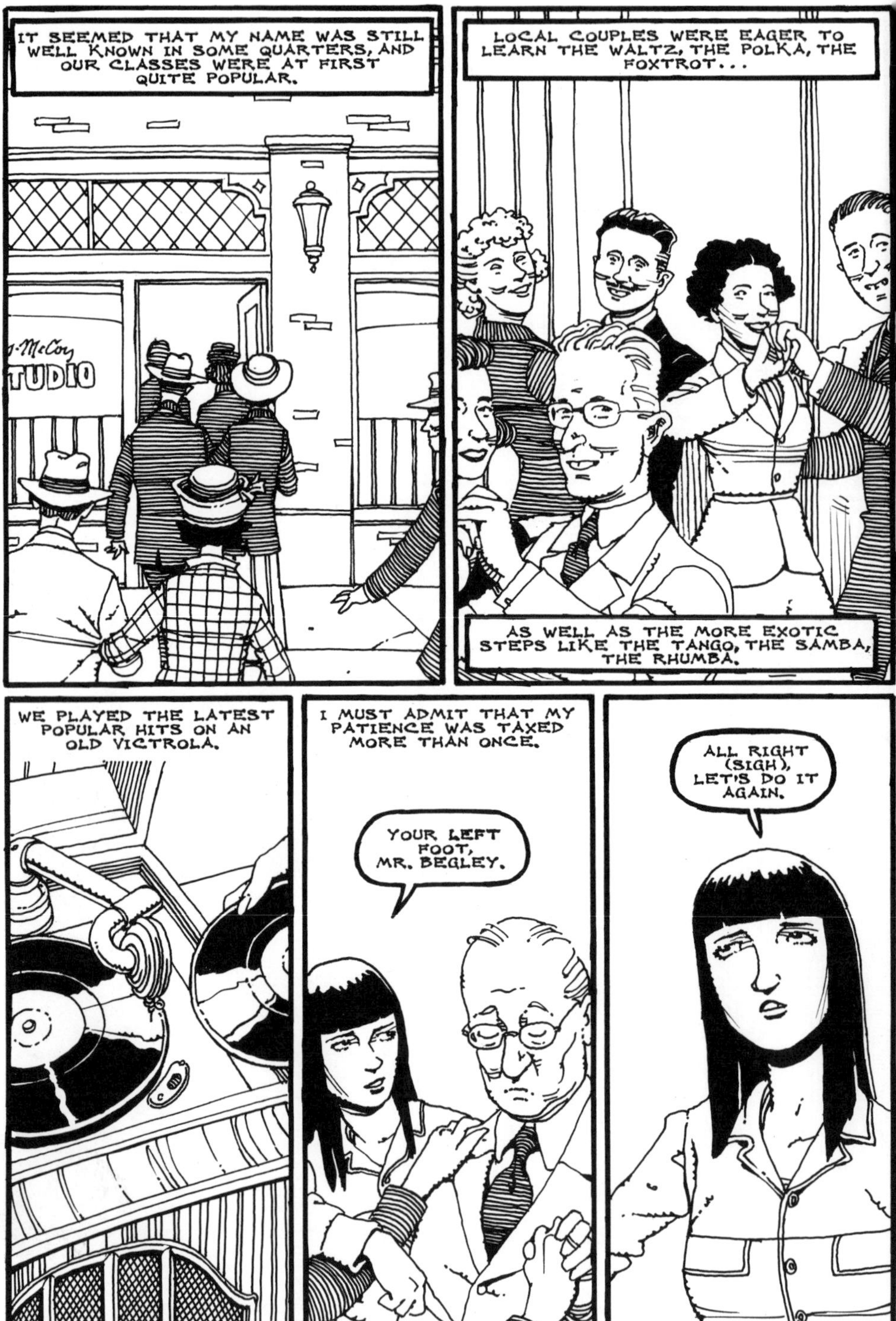
IT SEEMED THAT MY NAME WAS STILL WELL KNOWN IN SOME QUARTERS, AND OUR CLASSES WERE AT FIRST QUITE POPULAR.
TUDIO
LOCAL COUPLES WERE EAGER TO LEARN THE WALTZ, THE POLKA, THE FOXTROT...
AS WELL AS THE MORE EXOTIC STEPS LIKE THE TANGO, THE SAMBA, THE RHUMBA.
WE PLAYED THE LATEST POPULAR HITS ON AN OLD VICTROLA.
I MUST ADMIT THAT MY PATIENCE WAS TAXED MORE THAN ONCE.
YOUR LEFT FOOT, MR. BEGLEY.
ALL RIGHT (SIGH), LET'S DO IT AGAIN.

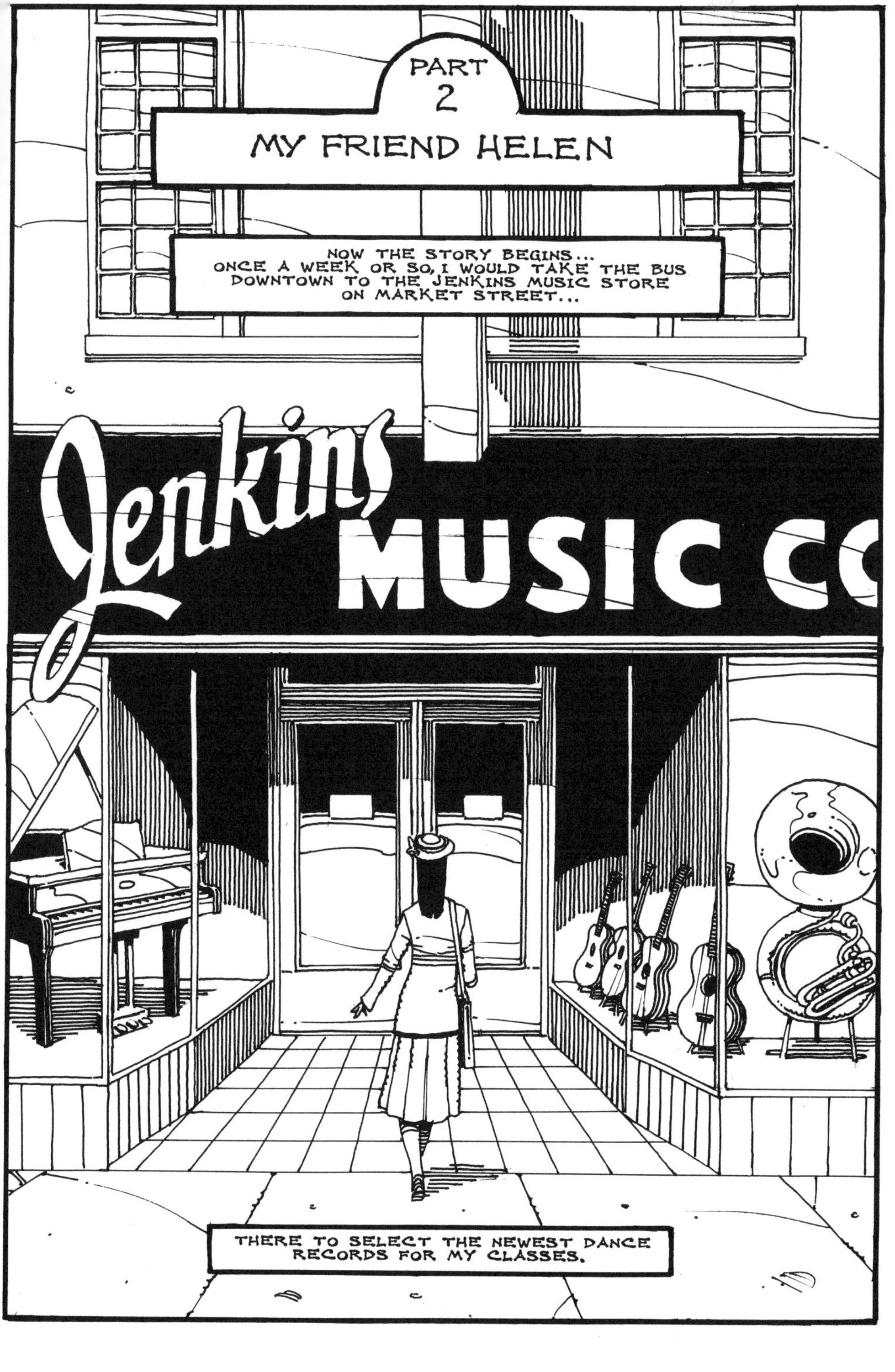
PART 2
MY FRIEND HELEN
NOW THE STORY BEGINS... ONCE A WEEK OR SO, I WOULD TAKE THE BUS DOWNTOWN TO THE JENKINS MUSIC STORE ON MARKET STREET...
Jenkins MUSIC CO
THERE TO SELECT THE NEWEST DANCE RECORDS FOR MY CLASSES.

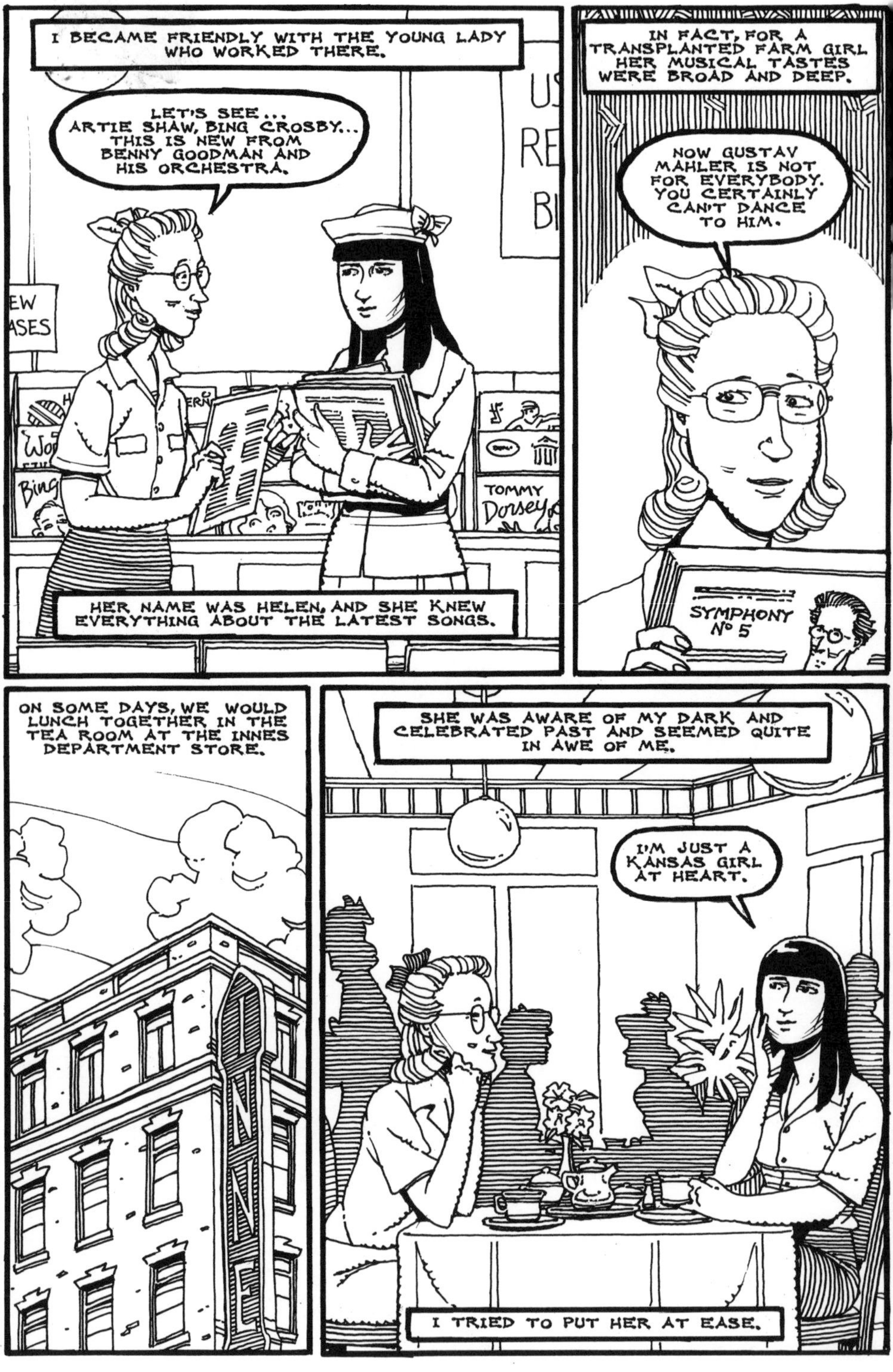
I BECAME FRIENDLY WITH THE YOUNG LADY WHO WORKED THERE.
LET'S SEE... ARTIE SHAW, BING CROSBY... THIS IS NEW FROM BENNY GOODMAN AND HIS ORCHESTRA.
HER NAME WAS HELEN, AND SHE KNEW EVERYTHING ABOUT THE LATEST SONGS.
TOMMY Dorsey
IN FACT, FOR A TRANSPLANTED FARM GIRL HER MUSICAL TASTES WERE BROAD AND DEEP.
NOW GUSTAV MAHLER IS NOT FOR EVERYBODY. YOU CERTAINLY CAN'T DANCE TO HIM.
SYMPHONY Nº 5
ON SOME DAYS, WE WOULD LUNCH TOGETHER IN THE TEA ROOM AT THE INNES DEPARTMENT STORE.
SHE WAS AWARE OF MY DARK AND CELEBRATED PAST AND SEEMED QUITE IN AWE OF ME.
I'M JUST A KANSAS GIRL AT HEART.
I TRIED TO PUT HER AT EASE.

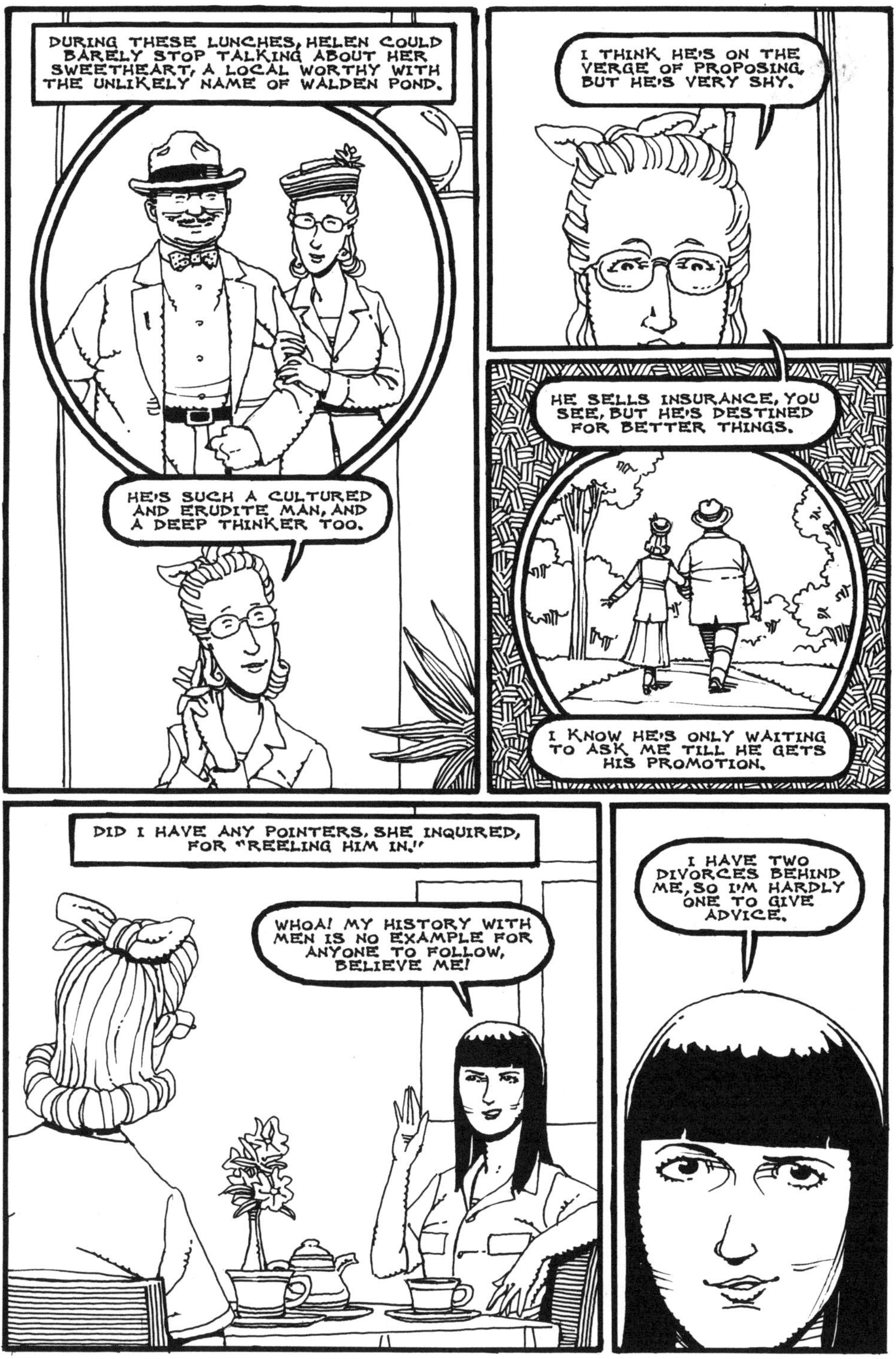
DURING THESE LUNCHES, HELEN COULD BARELY STOP TALKING ABOUT HER SWEETHEART, A LOCAL WORTHY WITH THE UNLIKELY NAME OF WALDEN POND.
HE'S SUCH A CULTURED AND ERUDITE MAN, AND A DEEP THINKER TOO.
I THINK HE'S ON THE VERGE OF PROPOSING, BUT HE'S VERY SHY.
HE SELLS INSURANCE, YOU SEE, BUT HE'S DESTINED FOR BETTER THINGS.
I KNOW HE'S ONLY WAITING TO ASK ME TILL HE GETS HIS PROMOTION.
DID I HAVE ANY POINTERS, SHE INQUIRED, FOR "REELING HIM IN."
WHOA! MY HISTORY WITH MEN IS NO EXAMPLE FOR ANYONE TO FOLLOW, BELIEVE ME!
I HAVE TWO DIVORCES BEHIND ME, SO I'M HARDLY ONE TO GIVE ADVICE.

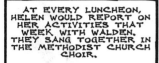

AT EVERY LUNCHEON, HELEN WOULD REPORT ON HER ACTIVITIES THAT WEEK WITH WALDEN. THEY SANG TOGETHER IN THE METHODIST CHURCH CHOIR.

HE HAS A LOVELY TENOR --- LIKE AN ANGEL.

I MUST ADMIT THAT THIS OFTEN BECAME TEDIOUS.

BUT I FELT I MUST MAKE ALLOWANCES, FOR HELEN HAD APPARENTLY GROWN UP WITH LITTLE LOVE IN HER LIFE.

WALDEN WAS ALSO, IT SEEMED, A TALENTED THESPIAN, A STAR OF THE COMMUNITY THEATRE.

HE WAS THE LEAD IN "PRIVATE LIVES" THIS YEAR. I'M SURE YOU CAN APPRECIATE THAT.

AND HE'S A WONDERFUL MIMIC! HE CAN IMITATE ANYONE!

HE ALWAYS KEEPS ME LAUGHING!

YES, I CAN APPRECIATE THAT, I SAID TO MYSELF, AS I RECALLED ADORNING THE ARM OF NONE OTHER THAN CHARLIE CHAPLIN DURING MY EARLY HEADY DAYS IN NEW YORK.

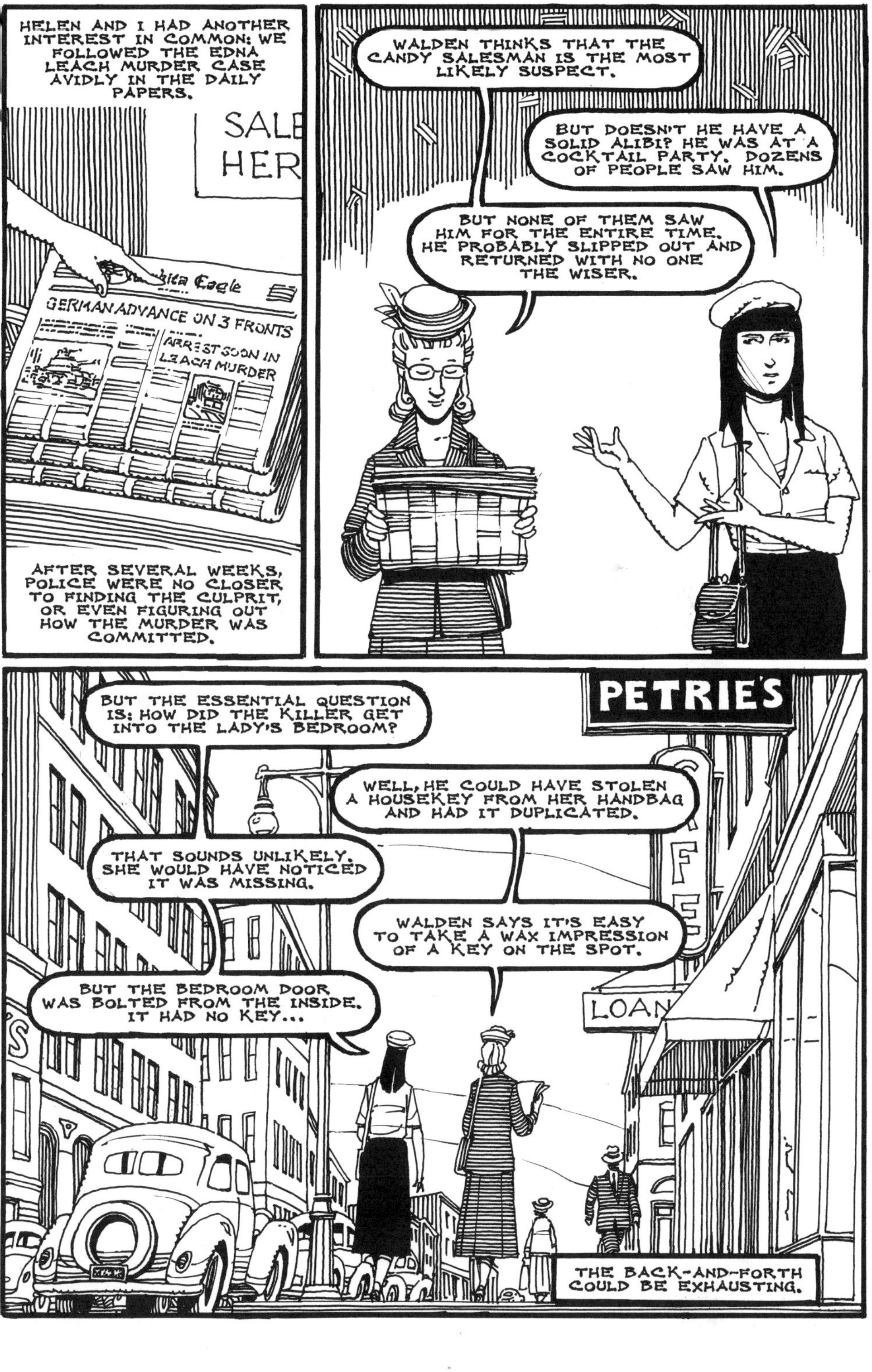
HELEN AND I HAD ANOTHER INTEREST IN COMMON: WE FOLLOWED THE EDNA LEACH MURDER CASE AVIDLY IN THE DAILY PAPERS.
SALE HER
GERMAN ADVANCE ON 3 FRONTS
ARREST SOON IN LEACH MURDER
AFTER SEVERAL WEEKS, POLICE WERE NO CLOSER TO FINDING THE CULPRIT, OR EVEN FIGURING OUT HOW THE MURDER WAS COMMITTED.
WALDEN THINKS THAT THE CANDY SALESMAN IS THE MOST LIKELY SUSPECT.
BUT DOESN'T HE HAVE A SOLID ALIBI? HE WAS AT A COCKTAIL PARTY. DOZENS OF PEOPLE SAW HIM.
BUT NONE OF THEM SAW HIM FOR THE ENTIRE TIME. HE PROBABLY SLIPPED OUT AND RETURNED WITH NO ONE THE WISER.
PETRIE'S
BUT THE ESSENTIAL QUESTION IS: HOW DID THE KILLER GET INTO THE LADY'S BEDROOM?
WELL, HE COULD HAVE STOLEN A HOUSEKEY FROM HER HANDBAG AND HAD IT DUPLICATED.
THAT SOUNDS UNLIKELY. SHE WOULD HAVE NOTICED IT WAS MISSING.
WALDEN SAYS IT'S EASY TO TAKE A WAX IMPRESSION OF A KEY ON THE SPOT.
BUT THE BEDROOM DOOR WAS BOLTED FROM THE INSIDE. IT HAD NO KEY...
LOAN
THE BACK-AND-FORTH COULD BE EXHAUSTING.

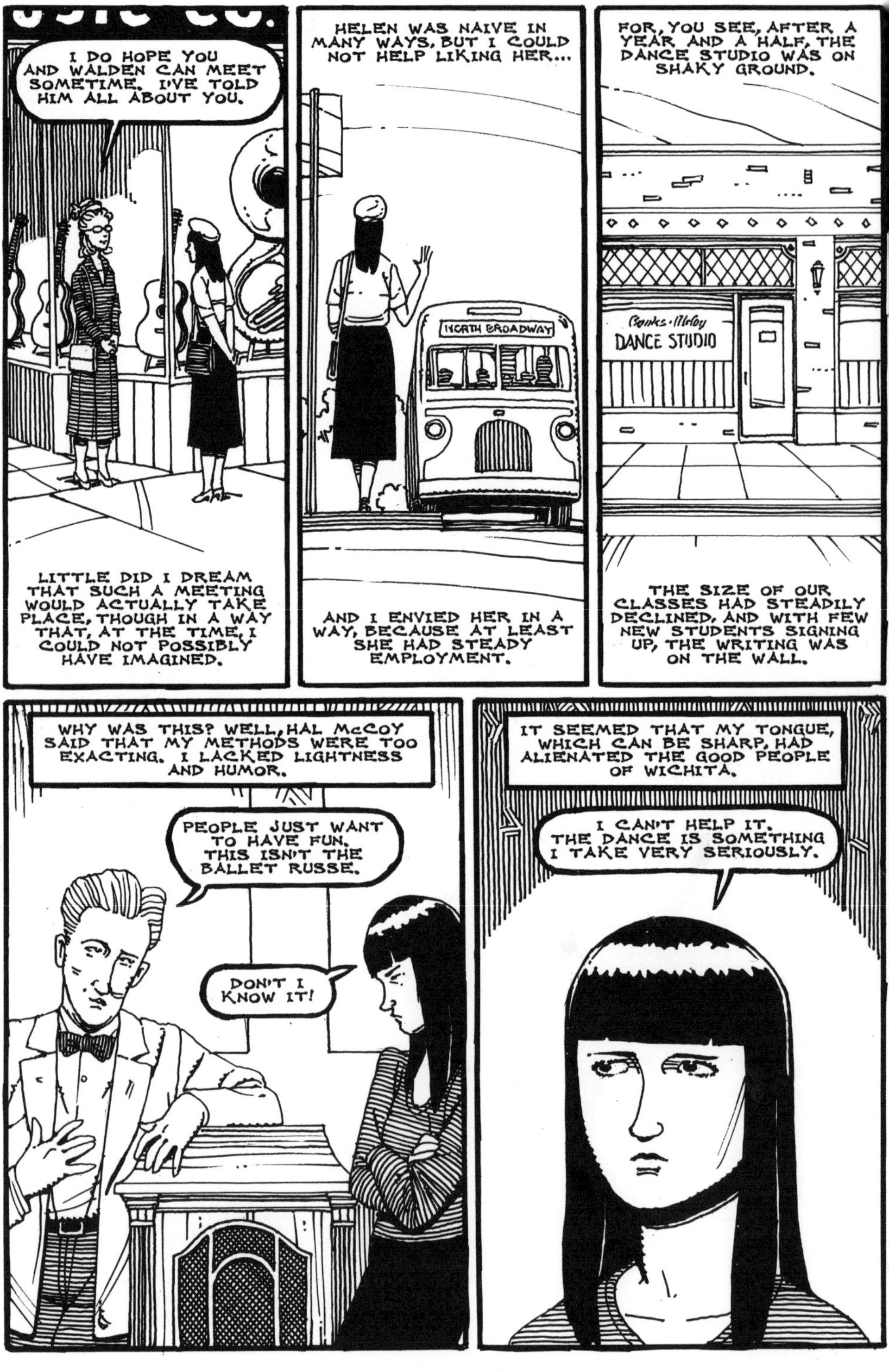
I DO HOPE YOU AND WALDEN CAN MEET SOMETIME. I'VE TOLD HIM ALL ABOUT YOU.
LITTLE DID I DREAM THAT SUCH A MEETING WOULD ACTUALLY TAKE PLACE, THOUGH IN A WAY THAT, AT THE TIME, I COULD NOT POSSIBLY HAVE IMAGINED.
HELEN WAS NAIVE IN MANY WAYS, BUT I COULD NOT HELP LIKING HER...
NORTH BROADWAY
AND I ENVIED HER IN A WAY, BECAUSE AT LEAST SHE HAD STEADY EMPLOYMENT.
FOR, YOU SEE, AFTER A YEAR AND A HALF, THE DANCE STUDIO WAS ON SHAKY GROUND.
Banks · McCoy
DANCE STUDIO
THE SIZE OF OUR CLASSES HAD STEADILY DECLINED, AND WITH FEW NEW STUDENTS SIGNING UP, THE WRITING WAS ON THE WALL.
WHY WAS THIS? WELL, HAL McCOY SAID THAT MY METHODS WERE TOO EXACTING. I LACKED LIGHTNESS AND HUMOR.
PEOPLE JUST WANT TO HAVE FUN. THIS ISN'T THE BALLET RUSSE.
DON'T I KNOW IT!
IT SEEMED THAT MY TONGUE, WHICH CAN BE SHARP, HAD ALIENATED THE GOOD PEOPLE OF WICHITA.
I CAN'T HELP IT. THE DANCE IS SOMETHING I TAKE VERY SERIOUSLY.

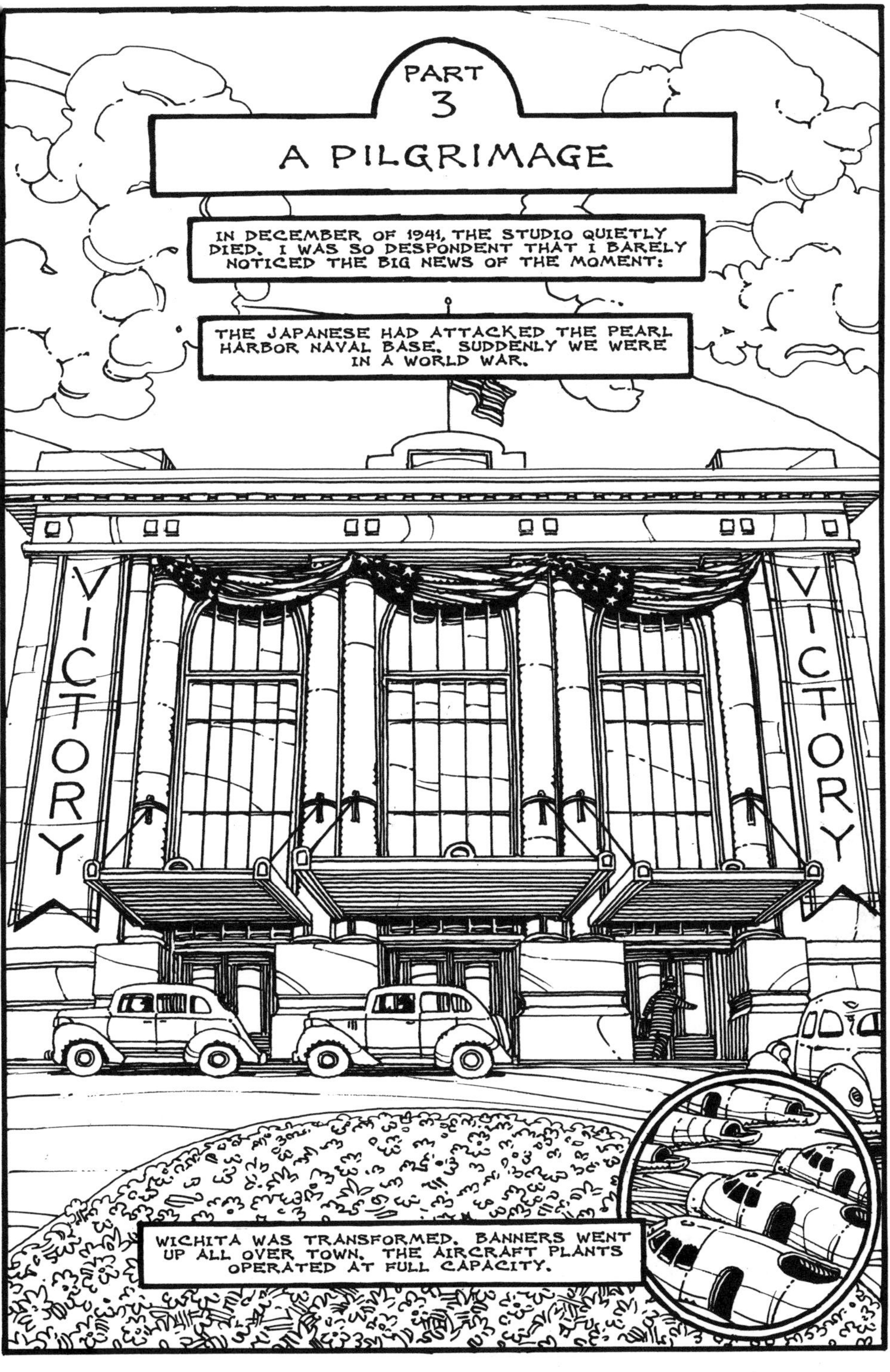
PART 3
A PILGRIMAGE
IN DECEMBER OF 1941, THE STUDIO QUIETLY DIED. I WAS SO DESPONDENT THAT I BARELY NOTICED THE BIG NEWS OF THE MOMENT:
THE JAPANESE HAD ATTACKED THE PEARL HARBOR NAVAL BASE. SUDDENLY WE WERE IN A WORLD WAR.
VICTORY
VICTORY
WICHITA WAS TRANSFORMED. BANNERS WENT UP ALL OVER TOWN. THE AIRCRAFT PLANTS OPERATED AT FULL CAPACITY.

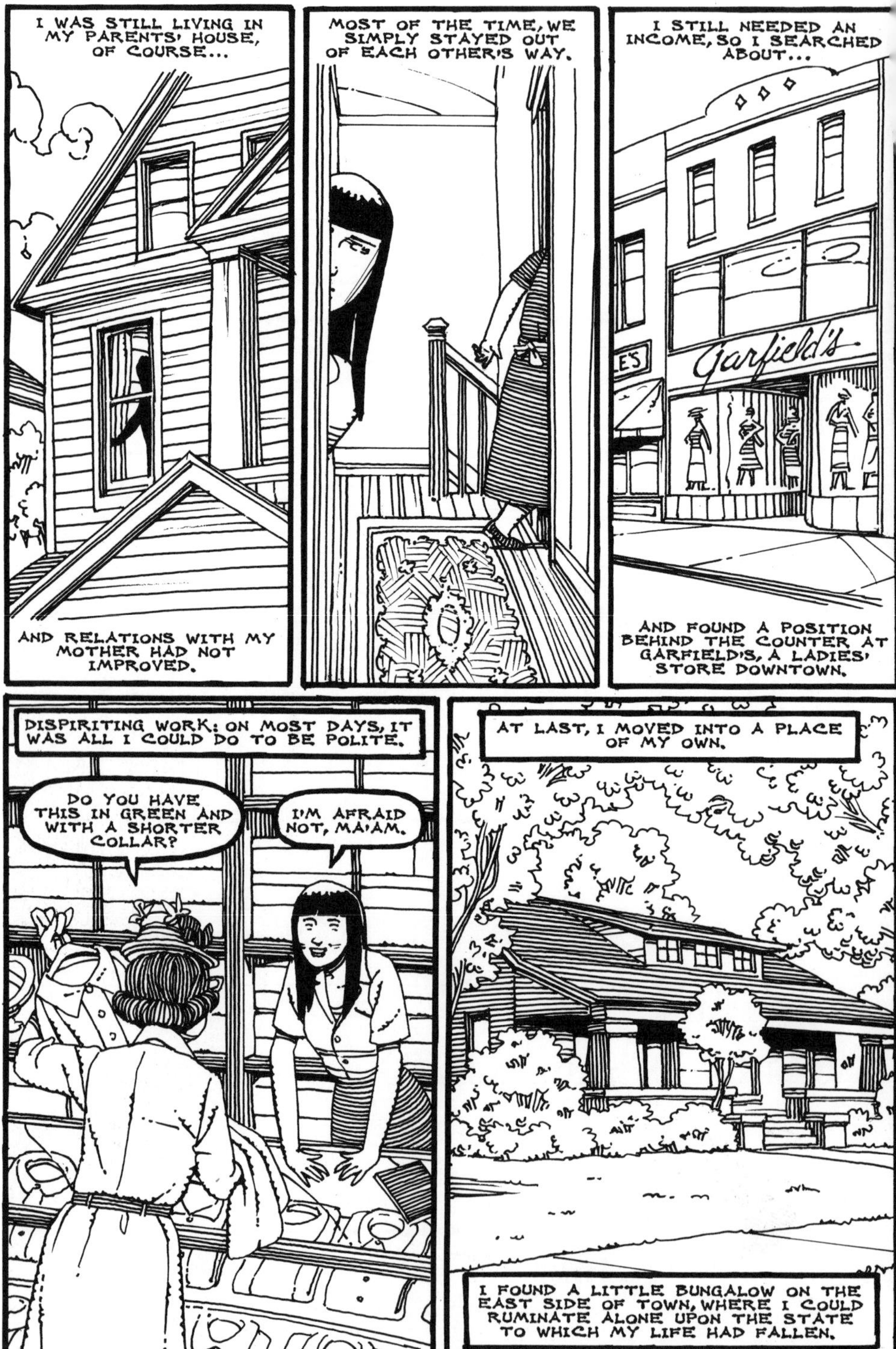
I WAS STILL LIVING IN MY PARENTS' HOUSE, OF COURSE...
AND RELATIONS WITH MY MOTHER HAD NOT IMPROVED.
MOST OF THE TIME, WE SIMPLY STAYED OUT OF EACH OTHER'S WAY.
I STILL NEEDED AN INCOME, SO I SEARCHED ABOUT...
Garfield's
AND FOUND A POSITION BEHIND THE COUNTER AT GARFIELD'S, A LADIES' STORE DOWNTOWN.
DISPIRITING WORK: ON MOST DAYS, IT WAS ALL I COULD DO TO BE POLITE.
DO YOU HAVE THIS IN GREEN AND WITH A SHORTER COLLAR?
I'M AFRAID NOT, MA'AM.
AT LAST, I MOVED INTO A PLACE OF MY OWN.
I FOUND A LITTLE BUNGALOW ON THE EAST SIDE OF TOWN, WHERE I COULD RUMINATE ALONE UPON THE STATE TO WHICH MY LIFE HAD FALLEN.

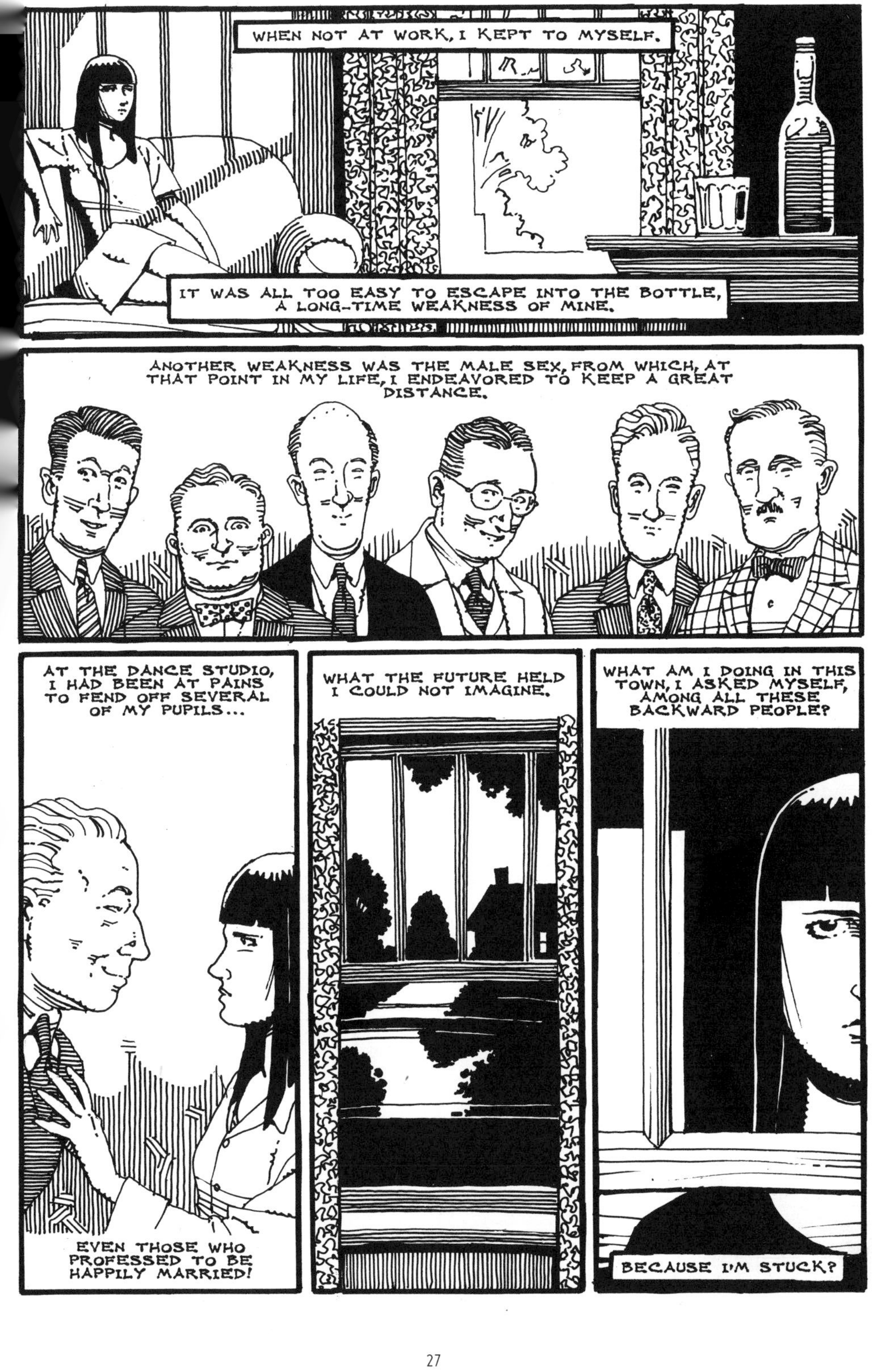
WHEN NOT AT WORK, I KEPT TO MYSELF.
IT WAS ALL TOO EASY TO ESCAPE INTO THE BOTTLE, A LONG-TIME WEAKNESS OF MINE.
ANOTHER WEAKNESS WAS THE MALE SEX, FROM WHICH, AT THAT POINT IN MY LIFE, I ENDEAVORED TO KEEP A GREAT DISTANCE.
AT THE DANCE STUDIO, I HAD BEEN AT PAINS TO FEND OFF SEVERAL OF MY PUPILS...
EVEN THOSE WHO PROFESSED TO BE HAPPILY MARRIED!
WHAT THE FUTURE HELD I COULD NOT IMAGINE.
WHAT AM I DOING IN THIS TOWN, I ASKED MYSELF, AMONG ALL THESE BACKWARD PEOPLE?
BECAUSE I'M STUCK?

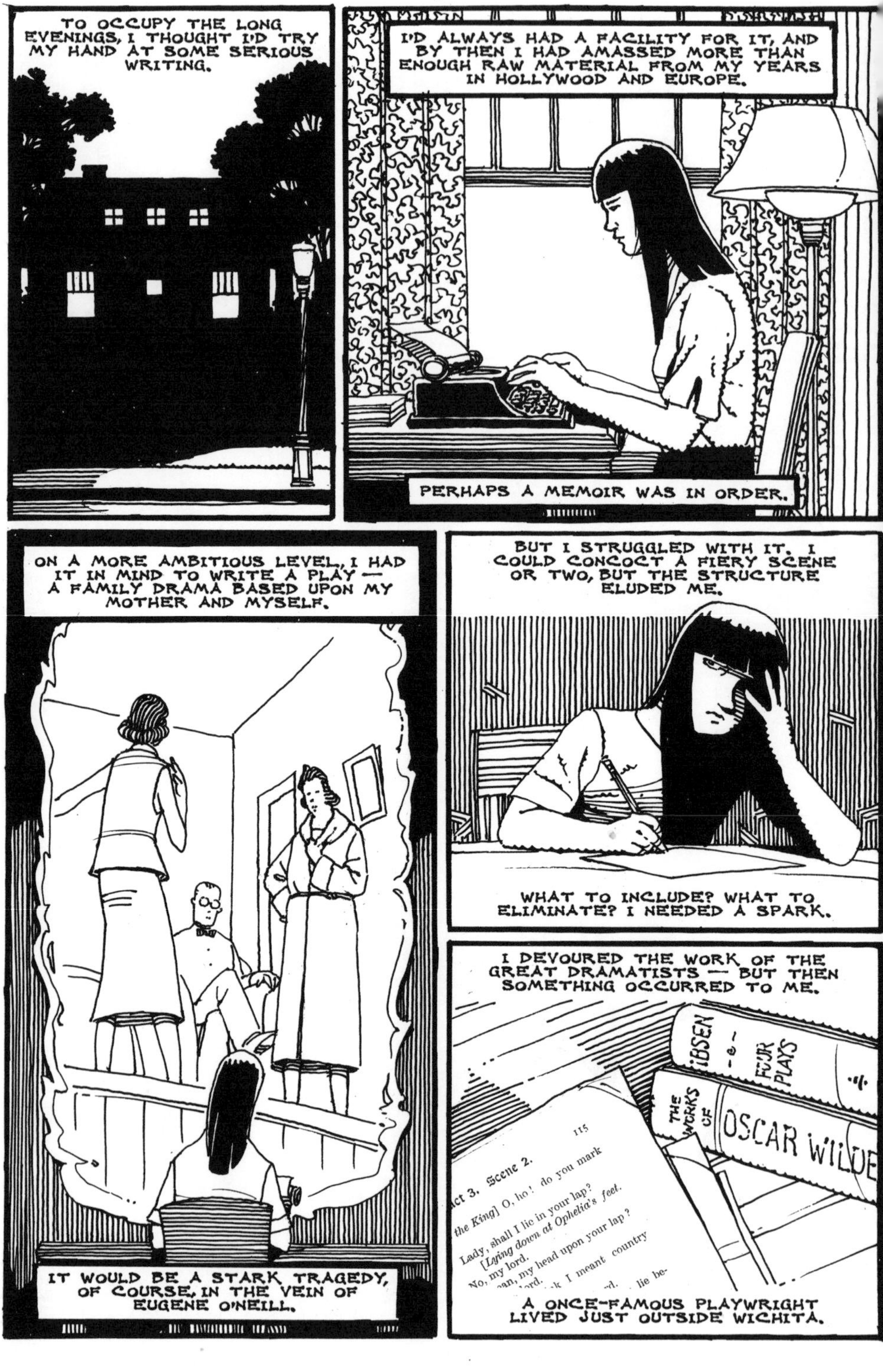
TO OCCUPY THE LONG EVENINGS, I THOUGHT I'D TRY MY HAND AT SOME SERIOUS WRITING.
I'D ALWAYS HAD A FACILITY FOR IT, AND BY THEN I HAD AMASSED MORE THAN ENOUGH RAW MATERIAL FROM MY YEARS IN HOLLYWOOD AND EUROPE.
PERHAPS A MEMOIR WAS IN ORDER.
ON A MORE AMBITIOUS LEVEL, I HAD IT IN MIND TO WRITE A PLAY — A FAMILY DRAMA BASED UPON MY MOTHER AND MYSELF.
IT WOULD BE A STARK TRAGEDY, OF COURSE, IN THE VEIN OF EUGENE O'NEILL.
BUT I STRUGGLED WITH IT. I COULD CONCOCT A FIERY SCENE OR TWO, BUT THE STRUCTURE ELUDED ME.
WHAT TO INCLUDE? WHAT TO ELIMINATE? I NEEDED A SPARK.
I DEVOURED THE WORK OF THE GREAT DRAMATISTS — BUT THEN SOMETHING OCCURRED TO ME.
IBSEN — FOUR PLAYS
THE WORKS OF OSCAR WILDE
A ONCE-FAMOUS PLAYWRIGHT LIVED JUST OUTSIDE WICHITA.

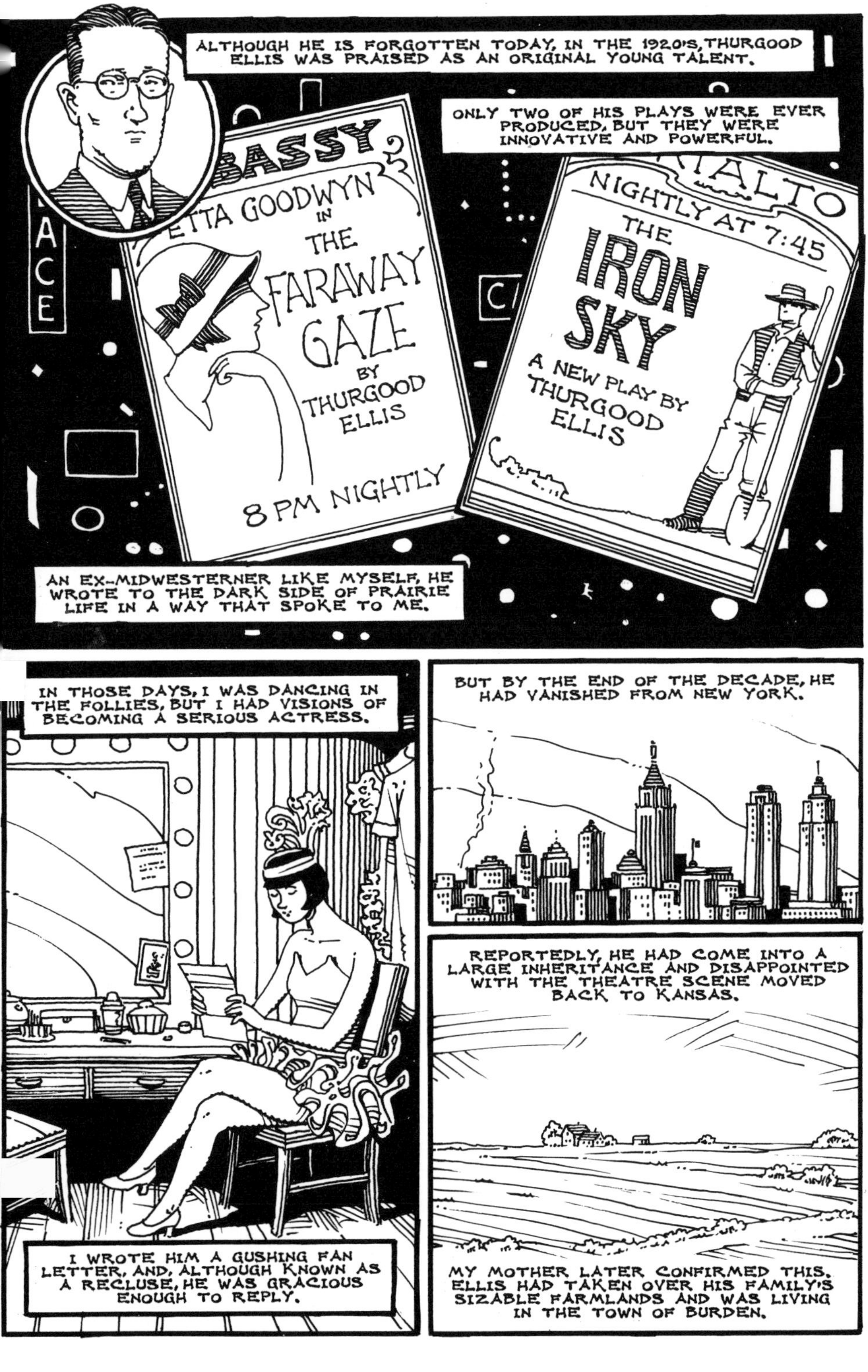

ALTHOUGH HE IS FORGOTTEN TODAY, IN THE 1920'S, THURGOOD ELLIS WAS PRAISED AS AN ORIGINAL YOUNG TALENT.
ONLY TWO OF HIS PLAYS WERE EVER PRODUCED, BUT THEY WERE INNOVATIVE AND POWERFUL.
ETTA GOODWYN IN THE FARAWAY GAZE BY THURGOOD ELLIS
8 PM NIGHTLY
NIGHTLY AT 7:45
THE IRON SKY
A NEW PLAY BY THURGOOD ELLIS
AN EX-MIDWESTERNER LIKE MYSELF, HE WROTE TO THE DARK SIDE OF PRAIRIE LIFE IN A WAY THAT SPOKE TO ME.
IN THOSE DAYS, I WAS DANCING IN THE FOLLIES, BUT I HAD VISIONS OF BECOMING A SERIOUS ACTRESS.
I WROTE HIM A GUSHING FAN LETTER, AND, ALTHOUGH KNOWN AS A RECLUSE, HE WAS GRACIOUS ENOUGH TO REPLY.
BUT BY THE END OF THE DECADE, HE HAD VANISHED FROM NEW YORK.
REPORTEDLY, HE HAD COME INTO A LARGE INHERITANCE AND DISAPPOINTED WITH THE THEATRE SCENE MOVED BACK TO KANSAS.
MY MOTHER LATER CONFIRMED THIS. ELLIS HAD TAKEN OVER HIS FAMILY'S SIZABLE FARMLANDS AND WAS LIVING IN THE TOWN OF BURDEN.

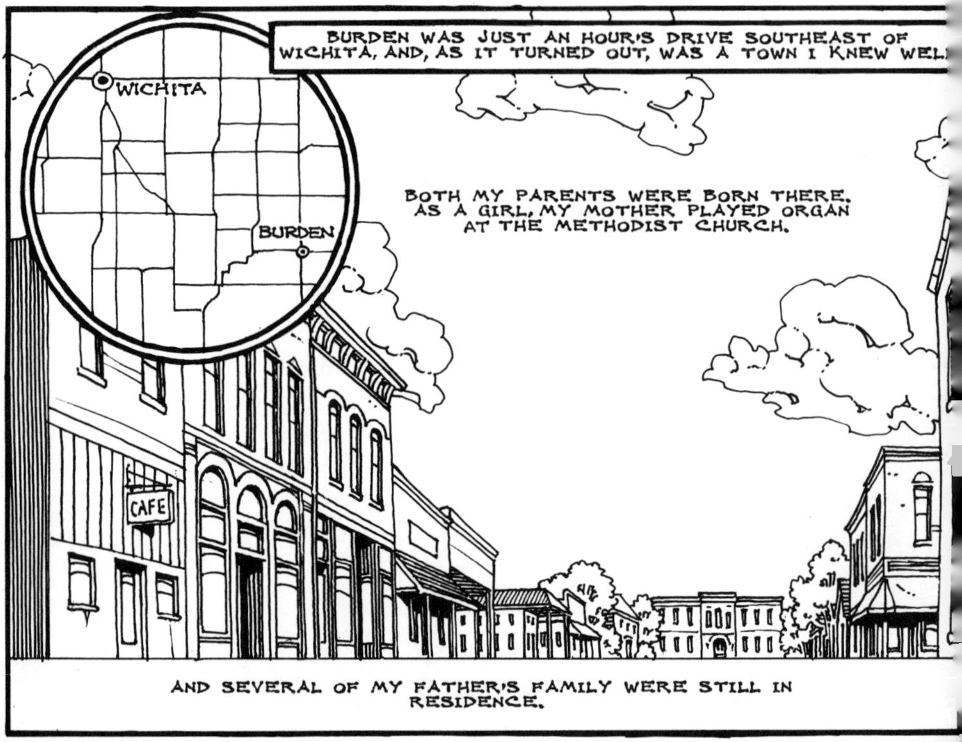
BURDEN WAS JUST AN HOUR'S DRIVE SOUTHEAST OF WICHITA, AND, AS IT TURNED OUT, WAS A TOWN I KNEW WELL
WICHITA
BURDEN
BOTH MY PARENTS WERE BORN THERE. AS A GIRL, MY MOTHER PLAYED ORGAN AT THE METHODIST CHURCH.
CAFE
AND SEVERAL OF MY FATHER'S FAMILY WERE STILL IN RESIDENCE.

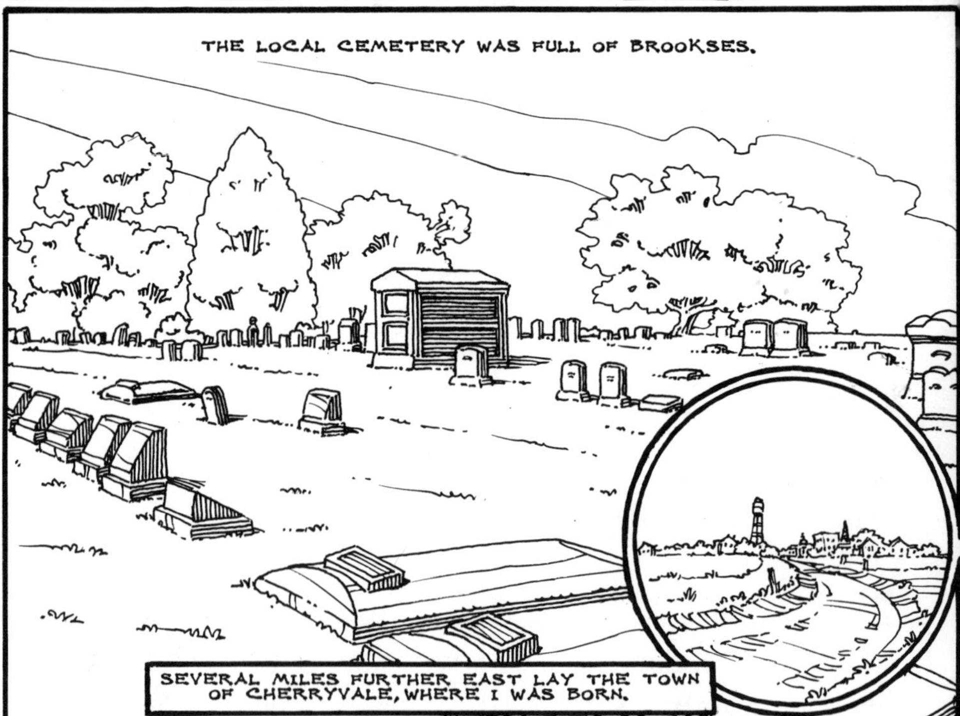
THE LOCAL CEMETERY WAS FULL OF BROOKSES.
SEVERAL MILES FURTHER EAST LAY THE TOWN OF CHERRYVALE, WHERE I WAS BORN.

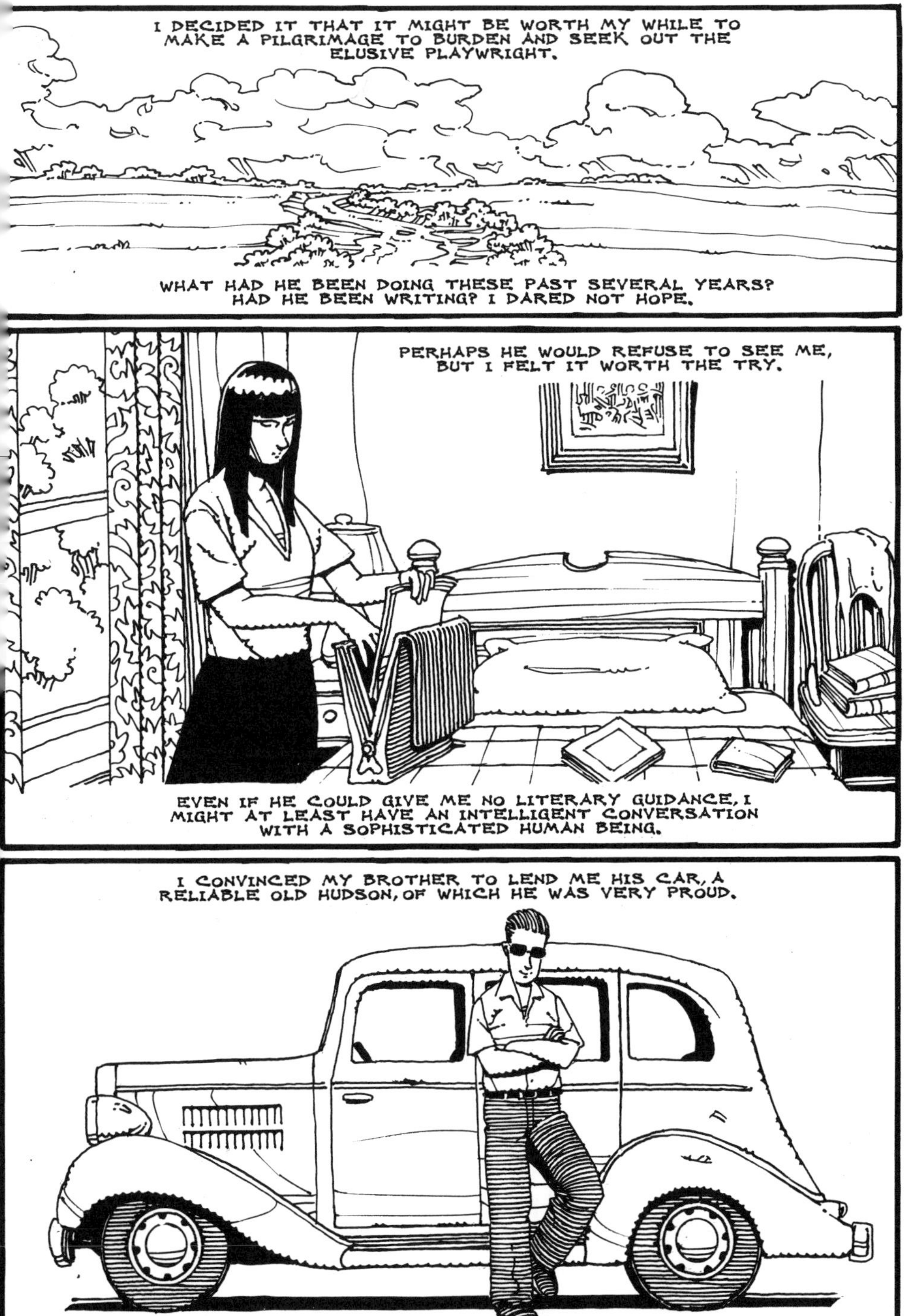
I DECIDED IT THAT IT MIGHT BE WORTH MY WHILE TO MAKE A PILGRIMAGE TO BURDEN AND SEEK OUT THE ELUSIVE PLAYWRIGHT.
WHAT HAD HE BEEN DOING THESE PAST SEVERAL YEARS? HAD HE BEEN WRITING? I DARED NOT HOPE.
PERHAPS HE WOULD REFUSE TO SEE ME, BUT I FELT IT WORTH THE TRY.
EVEN IF HE COULD GIVE ME NO LITERARY GUIDANCE, I MIGHT AT LEAST HAVE AN INTELLIGENT CONVERSATION WITH A SOPHISTICATED HUMAN BEING.
I CONVINCED MY BROTHER TO LEND ME HIS CAR, A RELIABLE OLD HUDSON, OF WHICH HE WAS VERY PROUD.
I PROMISED TO RETURN IT IN GOOD CONDITION.

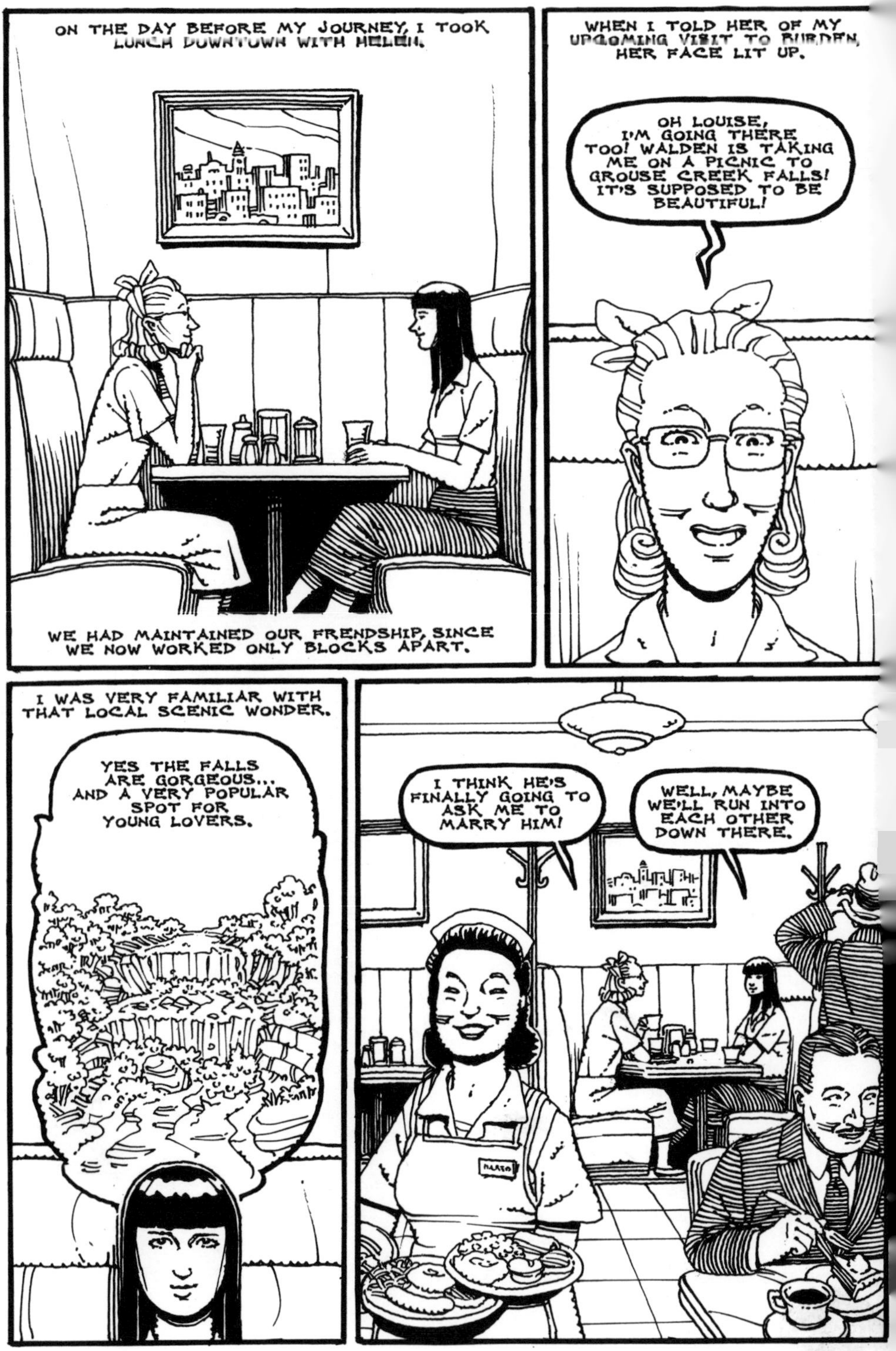
ON THE DAY BEFORE MY JOURNEY, I TOOK LUNCH DOWNTOWN WITH HELEN.
WE HAD MAINTAINED OUR FRENDSHIP, SINCE WE NOW WORKED ONLY BLOCKS APART.
WHEN I TOLD HER OF MY UPCOMING VISIT TO BURDEN, HER FACE LIT UP.
OH LOUISE, I'M GOING THERE TOO! WALDEN IS TAKING ME ON A PICNIC TO GROUSE CREEK FALLS! IT'S SUPPOSED TO BE BEAUTIFUL!
I WAS VERY FAMILIAR WITH THAT LOCAL SCENIC WONDER.
YES THE FALLS ARE GORGEOUS... AND A VERY POPULAR SPOT FOR YOUNG LOVERS.
I THINK HE'S FINALLY GOING TO ASK ME TO MARRY HIM!
WELL, MAYBE WE'LL RUN INTO EACH OTHER DOWN THERE.

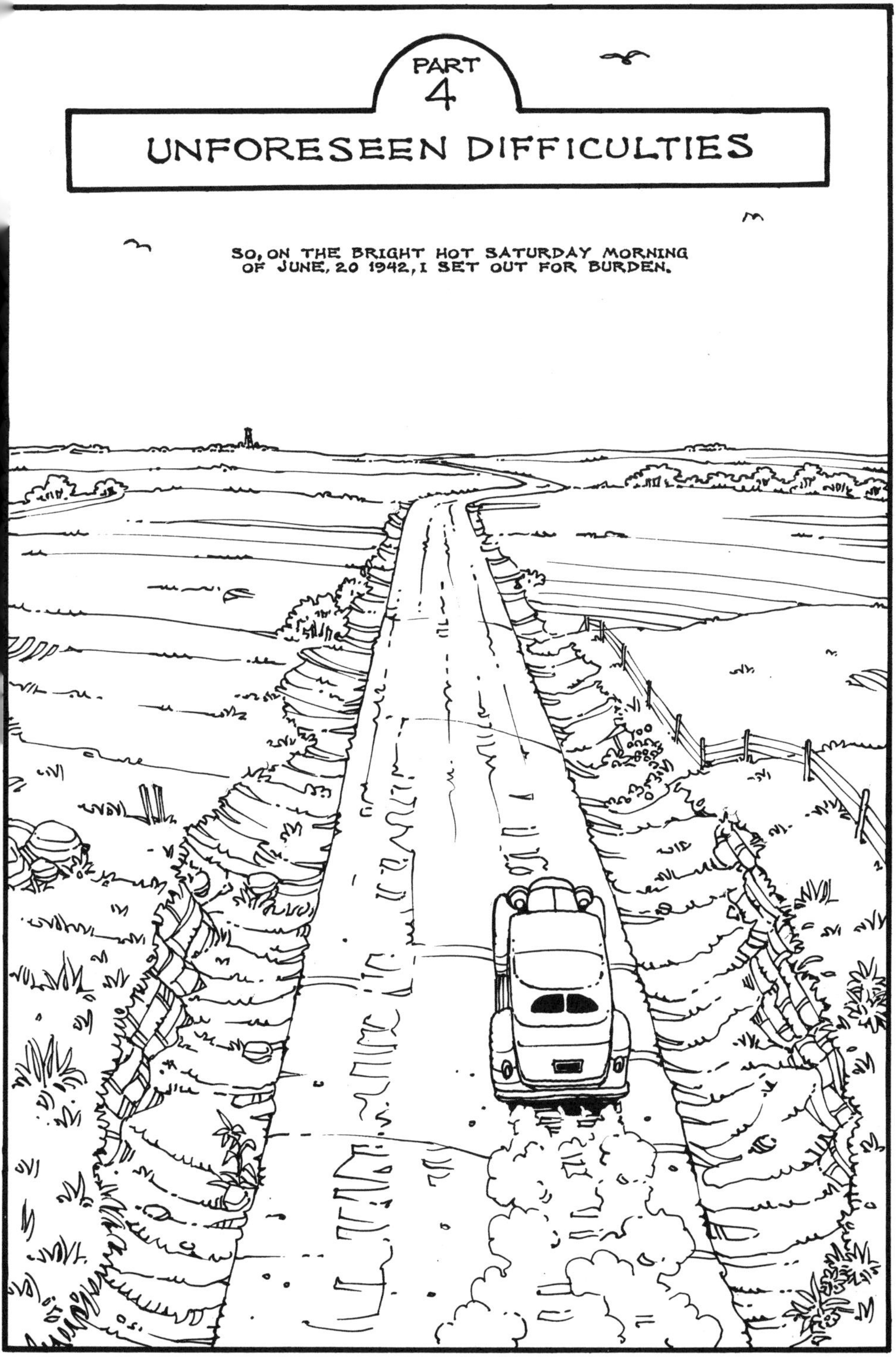
PART
4
UNFORESEEN DIFFICULTIES
SO, ON THE BRIGHT HOT SATURDAY MORNING OF JUNE, 20 1942, I SET OUT FOR BURDEN.

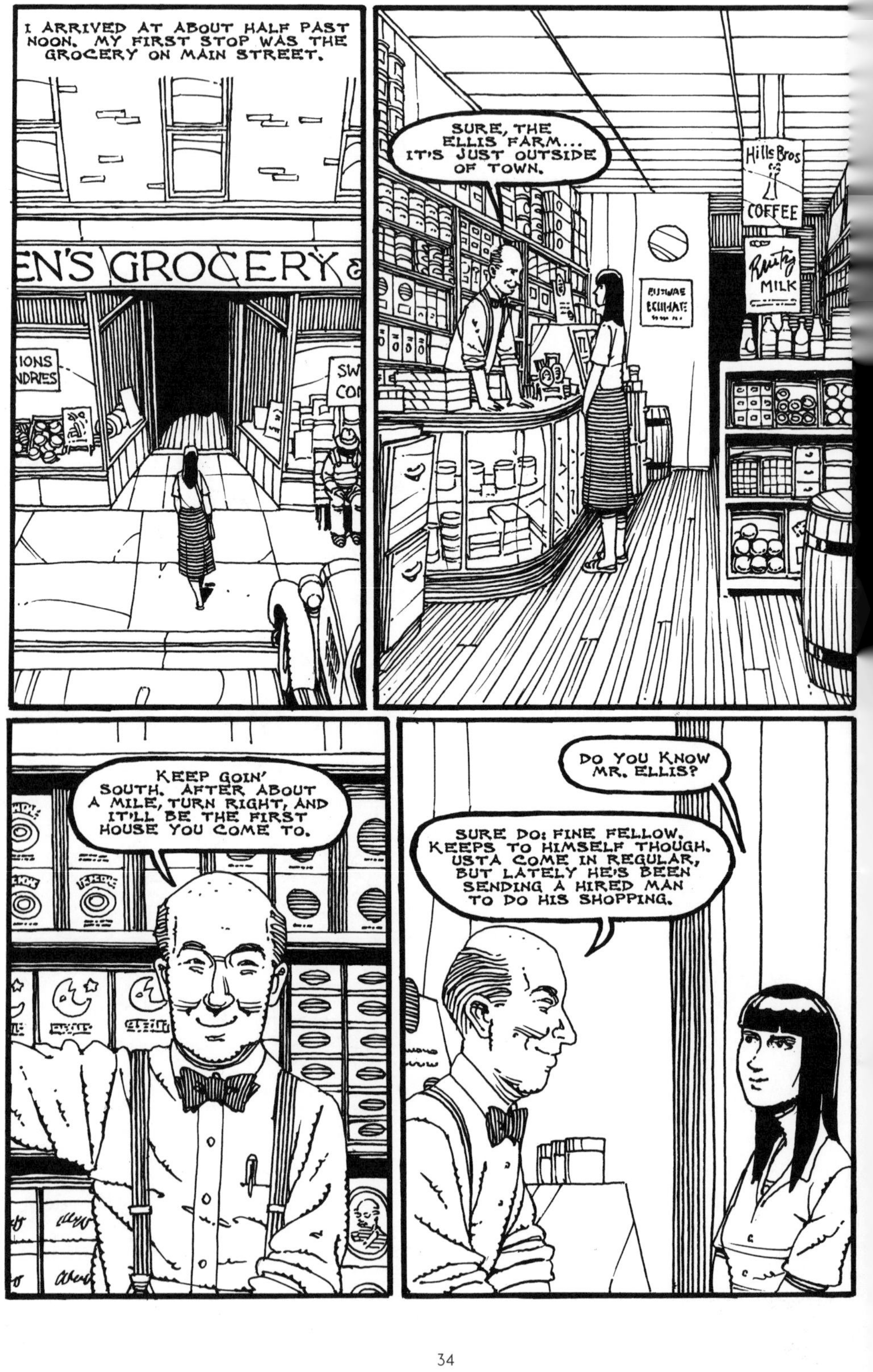
I ARRIVED AT ABOUT HALF PAST NOON. MY FIRST STOP WAS THE GROCERY ON MAIN STREET.
EN'S GROCERY
SURE, THE ELLIS FARM... IT'S JUST OUTSIDE OF TOWN.
Hills Bros COFFEE
MILK
KEEP GOIN' SOUTH. AFTER ABOUT A MILE, TURN RIGHT, AND IT'LL BE THE FIRST HOUSE YOU COME TO.
DO YOU KNOW MR. ELLIS?
SURE DO: FINE FELLOW. KEEPS TO HIMSELF THOUGH. USTA COME IN REGULAR, BUT LATELY HE'S BEEN SENDING A HIRED MAN TO DO HIS SHOPPING.

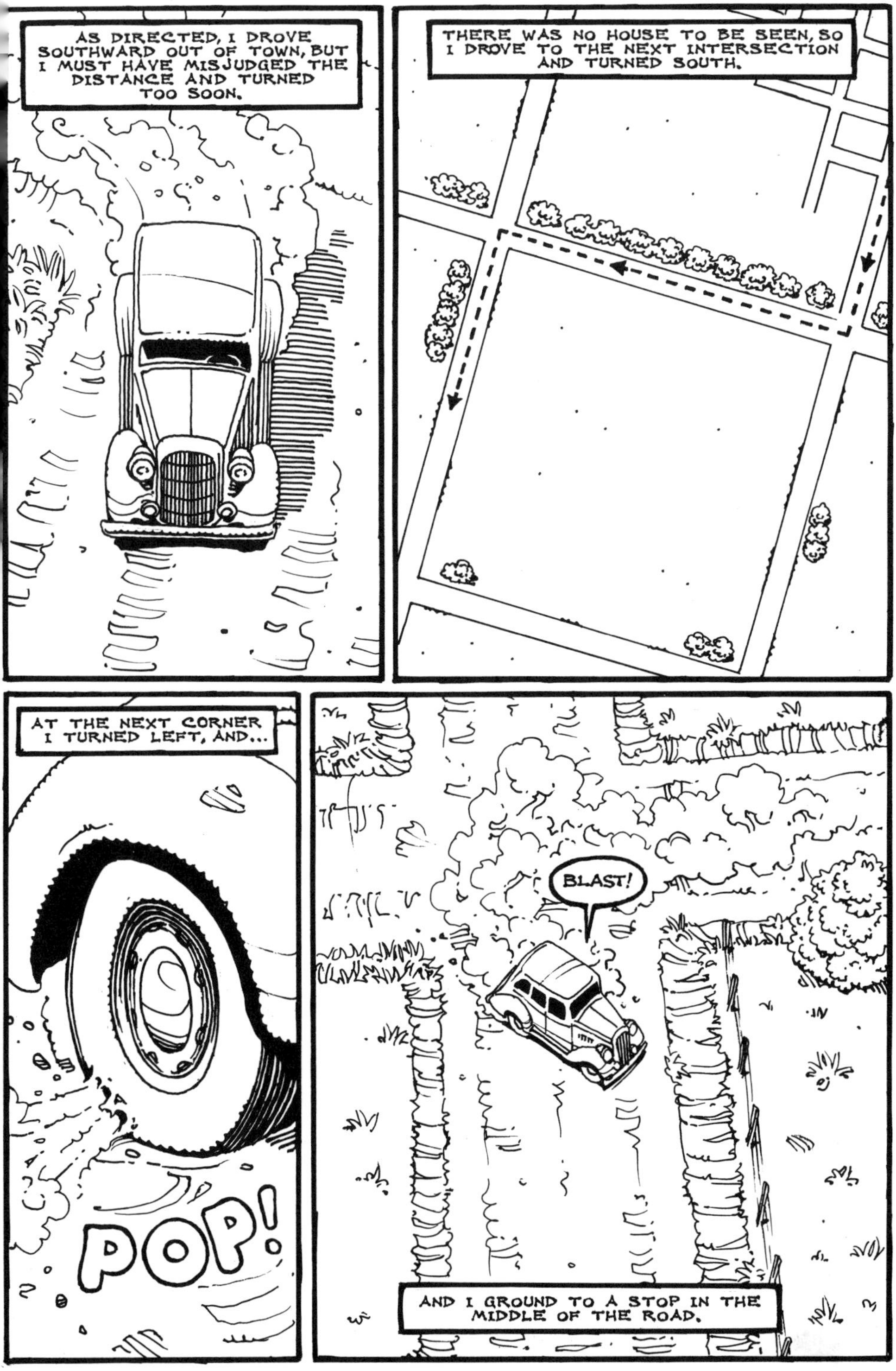
AS DIRECTED, I DROVE SOUTHWARD OUT OF TOWN, BUT I MUST HAVE MISJUDGED THE DISTANCE AND TURNED TOO SOON.
THERE WAS NO HOUSE TO BE SEEN, SO I DROVE TO THE NEXT INTERSECTION AND TURNED SOUTH.
AT THE NEXT CORNER I TURNED LEFT, AND...
POP!
BLAST!
AND I GROUND TO A STOP IN THE MIDDLE OF THE ROAD.

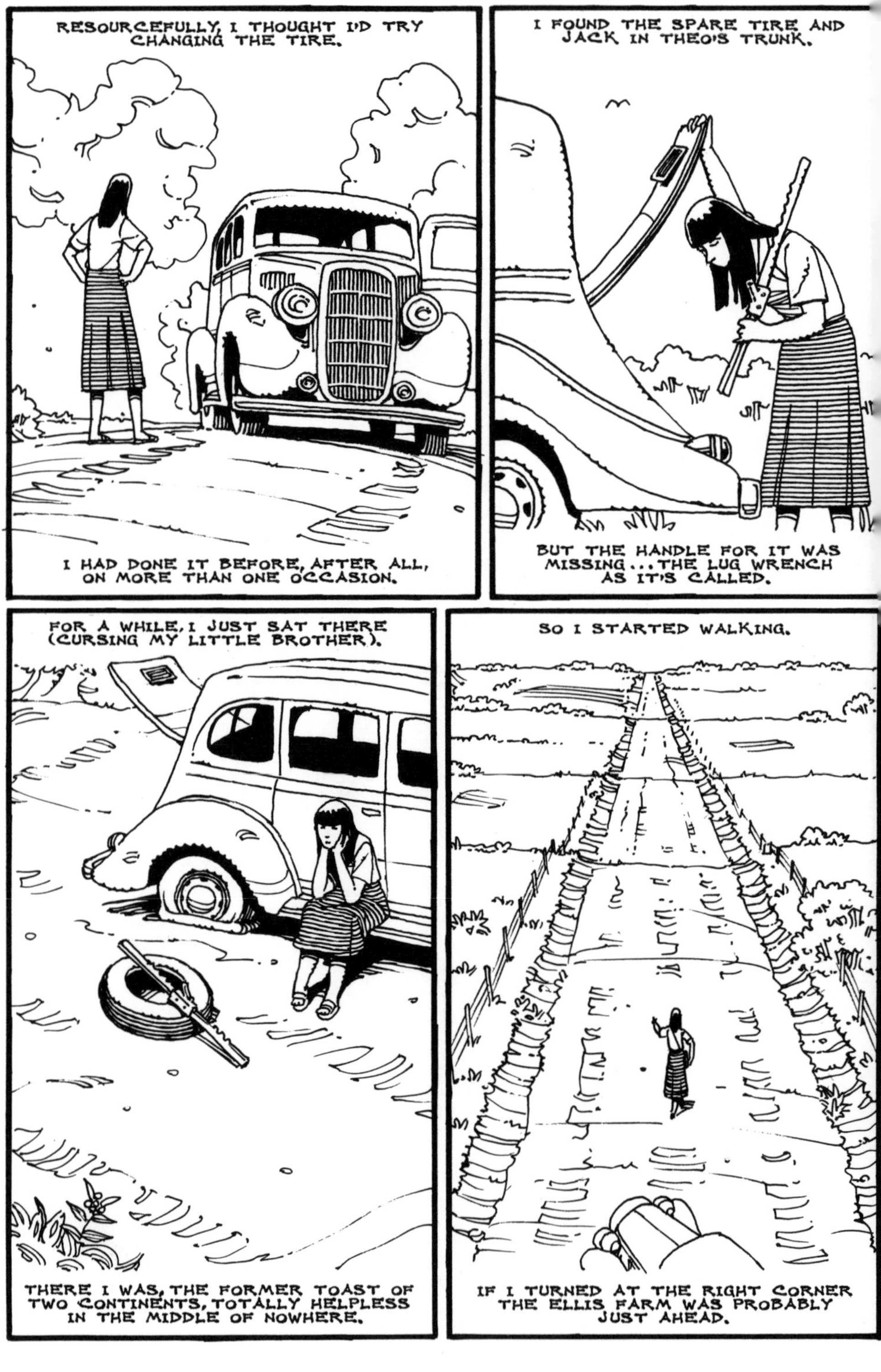
RESOURCEFULLY, I THOUGHT I'D TRY CHANGING THE TIRE.
I HAD DONE IT BEFORE, AFTER ALL, ON MORE THAN ONE OCCASION.
I FOUND THE SPARE TIRE AND JACK IN THEO'S TRUNK.
BUT THE HANDLE FOR IT WAS MISSING... THE LUG WRENCH AS IT'S CALLED.
FOR A WHILE, I JUST SAT THERE (CURSING MY LITTLE BROTHER).
THERE I WAS, THE FORMER TOAST OF TWO CONTINENTS, TOTALLY HELPLESS IN THE MIDDLE OF NOWHERE.
SO I STARTED WALKING.
IF I TURNED AT THE RIGHT CORNER THE ELLIS FARM WAS PROBABLY JUST AHEAD.

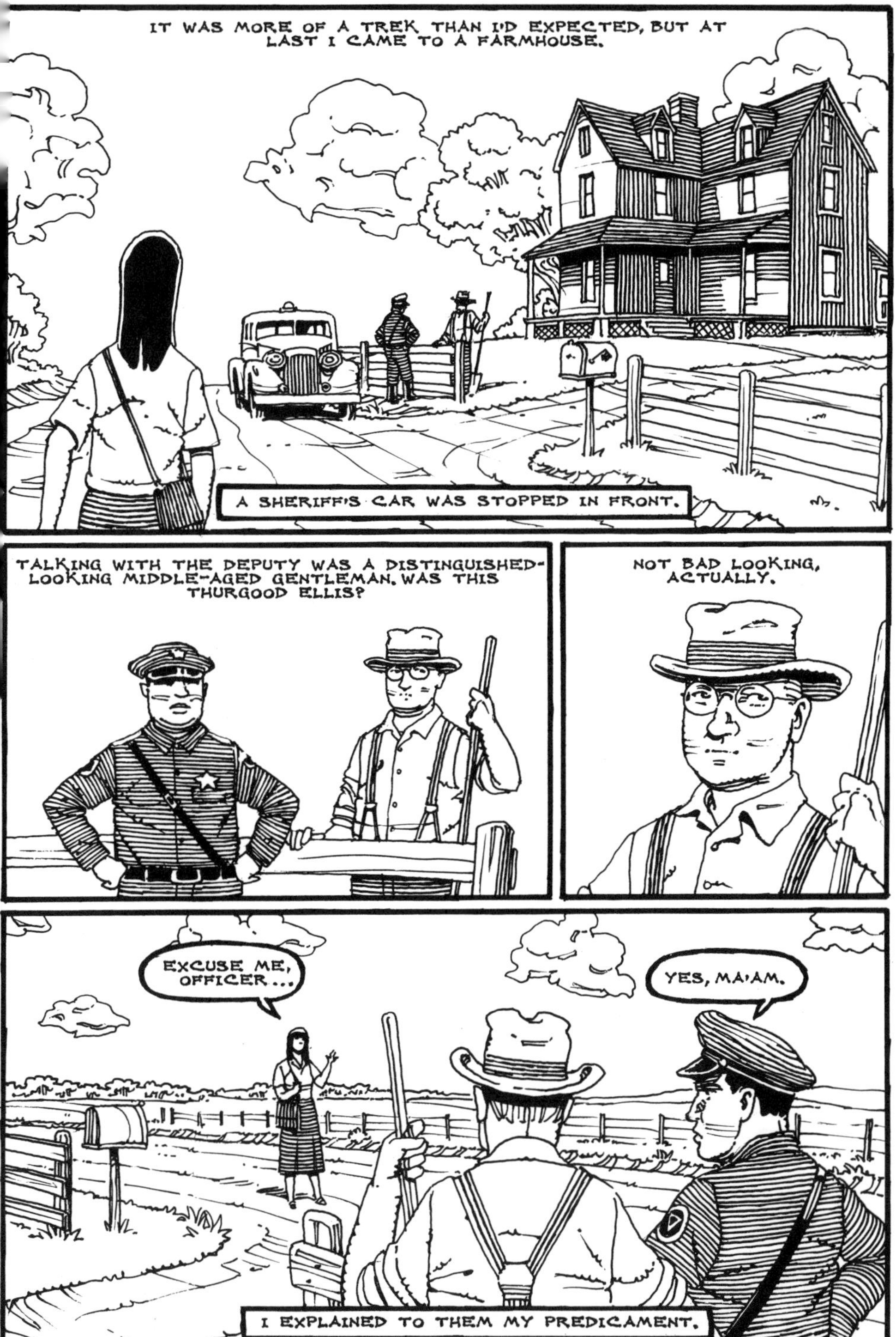
IT WAS MORE OF A TREK THAN I'D EXPECTED, BUT AT LAST I CAME TO A FARMHOUSE.
A SHERIFF'S CAR WAS STOPPED IN FRONT.
TALKING WITH THE DEPUTY WAS A DISTINGUISHED-LOOKING MIDDLE-AGED GENTLEMAN. WAS THIS THURGOOD ELLIS?
NOT BAD LOOKING, ACTUALLY.
EXCUSE ME, OFFICER...
YES, MA'AM.
I EXPLAINED TO THEM MY PREDICAMENT.

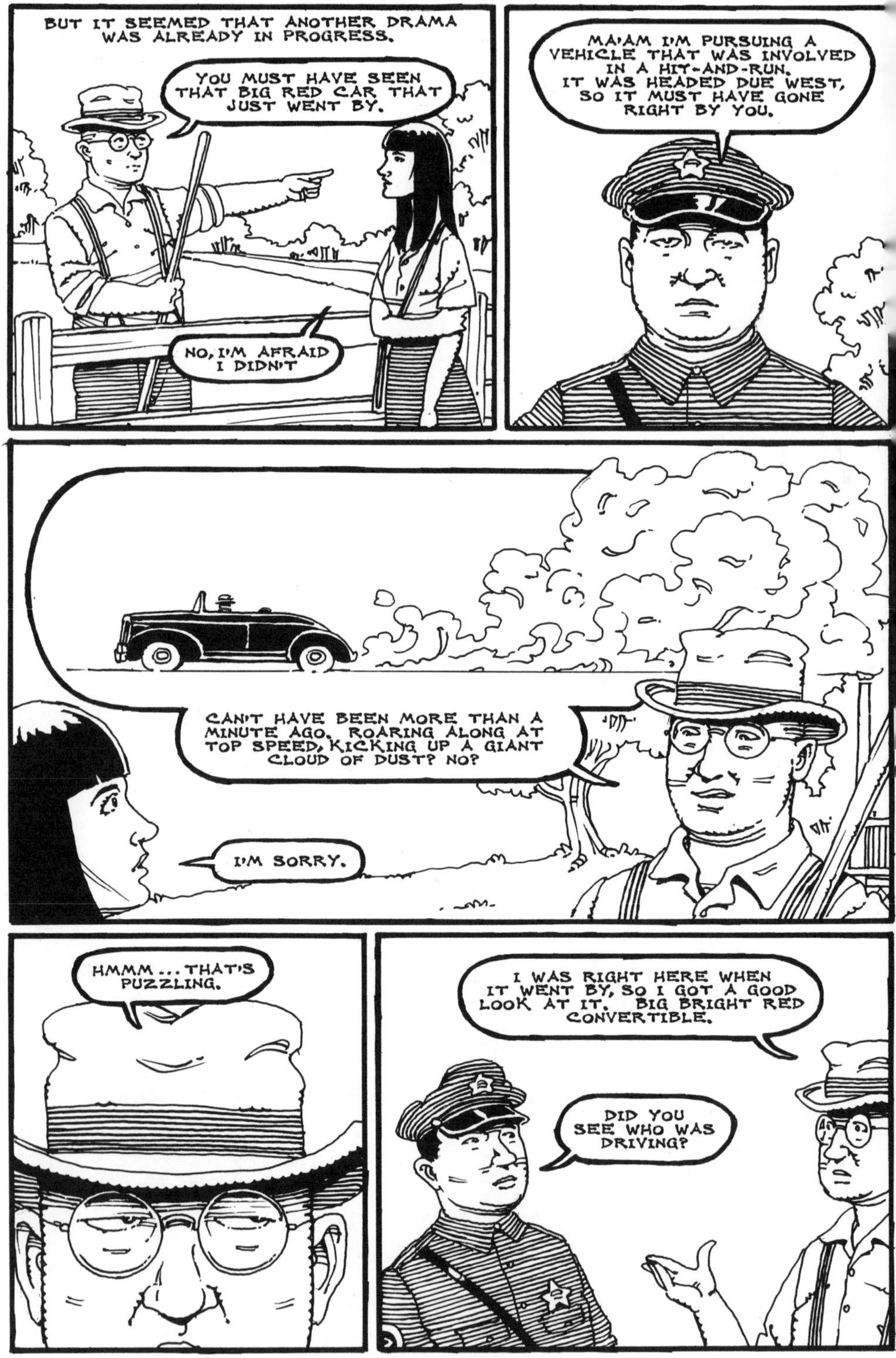

BUT IT SEEMED THAT ANOTHER DRAMA WAS ALREADY IN PROGRESS.
YOU MUST HAVE SEEN THAT BIG RED CAR THAT JUST WENT BY.
NO, I'M AFRAID I DIDN'T
MA'AM I'M PURSUING A VEHICLE THAT WAS INVOLVED IN A HIT-AND-RUN. IT WAS HEADED DUE WEST, SO IT MUST HAVE GONE RIGHT BY YOU.
CAN'T HAVE BEEN MORE THAN A MINUTE AGO. ROARING ALONG AT TOP SPEED, KICKING UP A GIANT CLOUD OF DUST? NO?
I'M SORRY.
HMMM... THAT'S PUZZLING.
I WAS RIGHT HERE WHEN IT WENT BY, SO I GOT A GOOD LOOK AT IT. BIG BRIGHT RED CONVERTIBLE.
DID YOU SEE WHO WAS DRIVING?

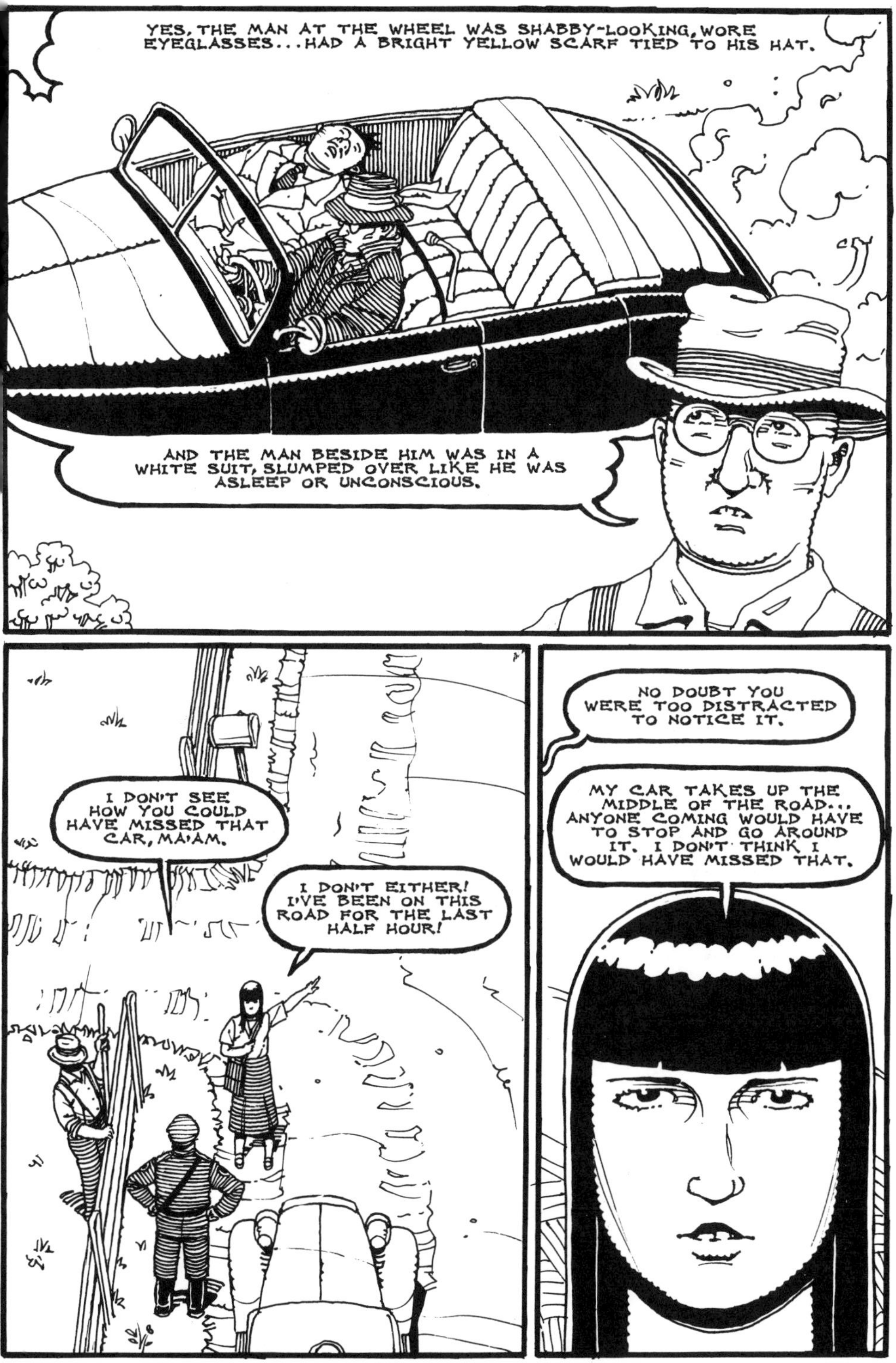
YES, THE MAN AT THE WHEEL WAS SHABBY-LOOKING, WORE EYEGLASSES...HAD A BRIGHT YELLOW SCARF TIED TO HIS HAT.
AND THE MAN BESIDE HIM WAS IN A WHITE SUIT, SLUMPED OVER LIKE HE WAS ASLEEP OR UNCONSCIOUS.
I DON'T SEE HOW YOU COULD HAVE MISSED THAT CAR, MA'AM.
I DON'T EITHER! I'VE BEEN ON THIS ROAD FOR THE LAST HALF HOUR!
NO DOUBT YOU WERE TOO DISTRACTED TO NOTICE IT.
MY CAR TAKES UP THE MIDDLE OF THE ROAD... ANYONE COMING WOULD HAVE TO STOP AND GO AROUND IT. I DON'T THINK I WOULD HAVE MISSED THAT.

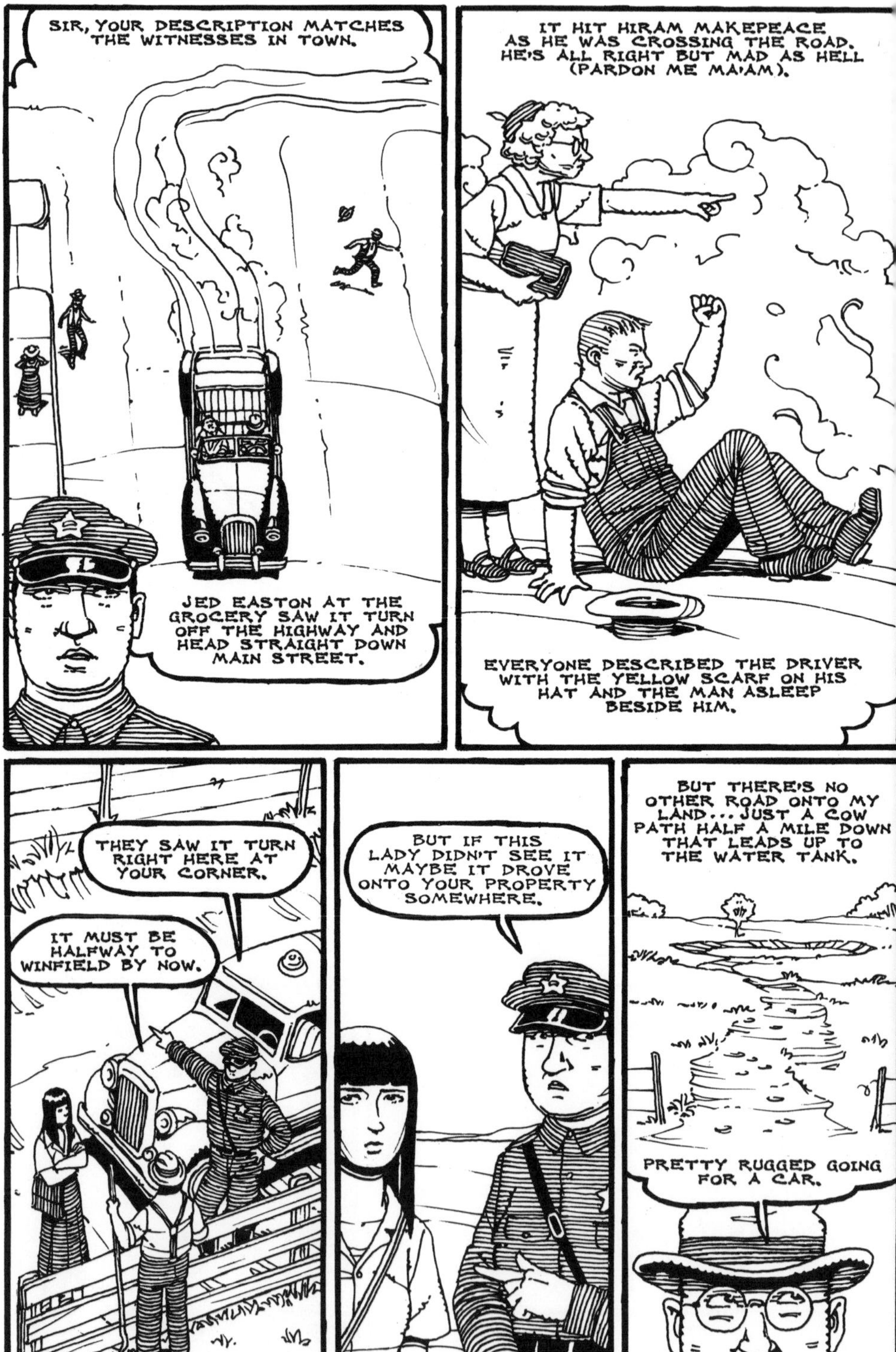
SIR, YOUR DESCRIPTION MATCHES THE WITNESSES IN TOWN.
JED EASTON AT THE GROCERY SAW IT TURN OFF THE HIGHWAY AND HEAD STRAIGHT DOWN MAIN STREET.
IT HIT HIRAM MAKEPEACE AS HE WAS CROSSING THE ROAD. HE'S ALL RIGHT BUT MAD AS HELL (PARDON ME MA'AM).
EVERYONE DESCRIBED THE DRIVER WITH THE YELLOW SCARF ON HIS HAT AND THE MAN ASLEEP BESIDE HIM.
THEY SAW IT TURN RIGHT HERE AT YOUR CORNER.
IT MUST BE HALFWAY TO WINFIELD BY NOW.
BUT IF THIS LADY DIDN'T SEE IT MAYBE IT DROVE ONTO YOUR PROPERTY SOMEWHERE.
BUT THERE'S NO OTHER ROAD ONTO MY LAND... JUST A COW PATH HALF A MILE DOWN THAT LEADS UP TO THE WATER TANK.
PRETTY RUGGED GOING FOR A CAR.

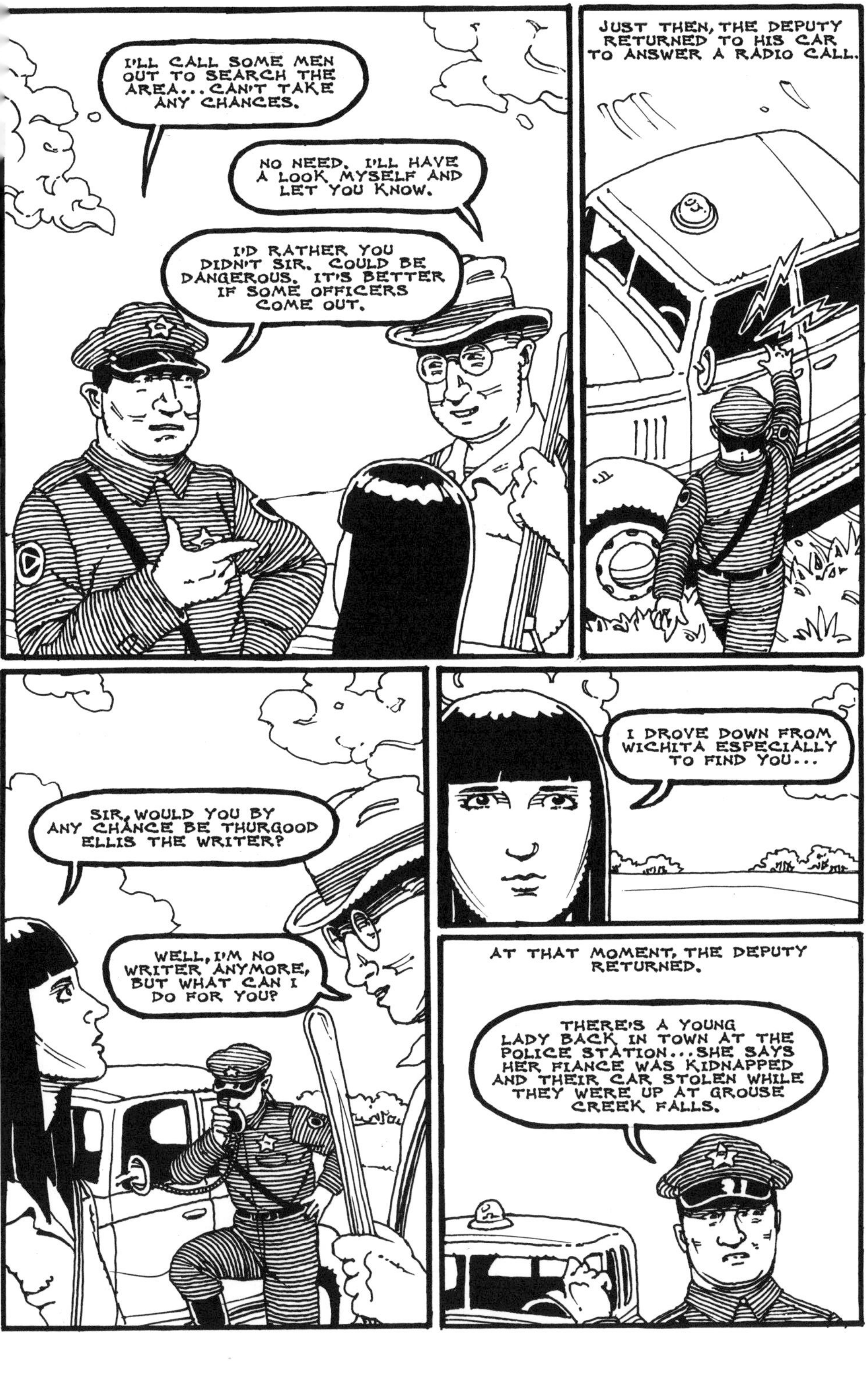

I'LL CALL SOME MEN OUT TO SEARCH THE AREA...CAN'T TAKE ANY CHANCES.
NO NEED. I'LL HAVE A LOOK MYSELF AND LET YOU KNOW.
I'D RATHER YOU DIDN'T SIR. COULD BE DANGEROUS. IT'S BETTER IF SOME OFFICERS COME OUT.
JUST THEN, THE DEPUTY RETURNED TO HIS CAR TO ANSWER A RADIO CALL.
SIR, WOULD YOU BY ANY CHANCE BE THURGOOD ELLIS THE WRITER?
WELL, I'M NO WRITER ANYMORE, BUT WHAT CAN I DO FOR YOU?
I DROVE DOWN FROM WICHITA ESPECIALLY TO FIND YOU...
AT THAT MOMENT, THE DEPUTY RETURNED.
THERE'S A YOUNG LADY BACK IN TOWN AT THE POLICE STATION...SHE SAYS HER FIANCE WAS KIDNAPPED AND THEIR CAR STOLEN WHILE THEY WERE UP AT GROUSE CREEK FALLS.

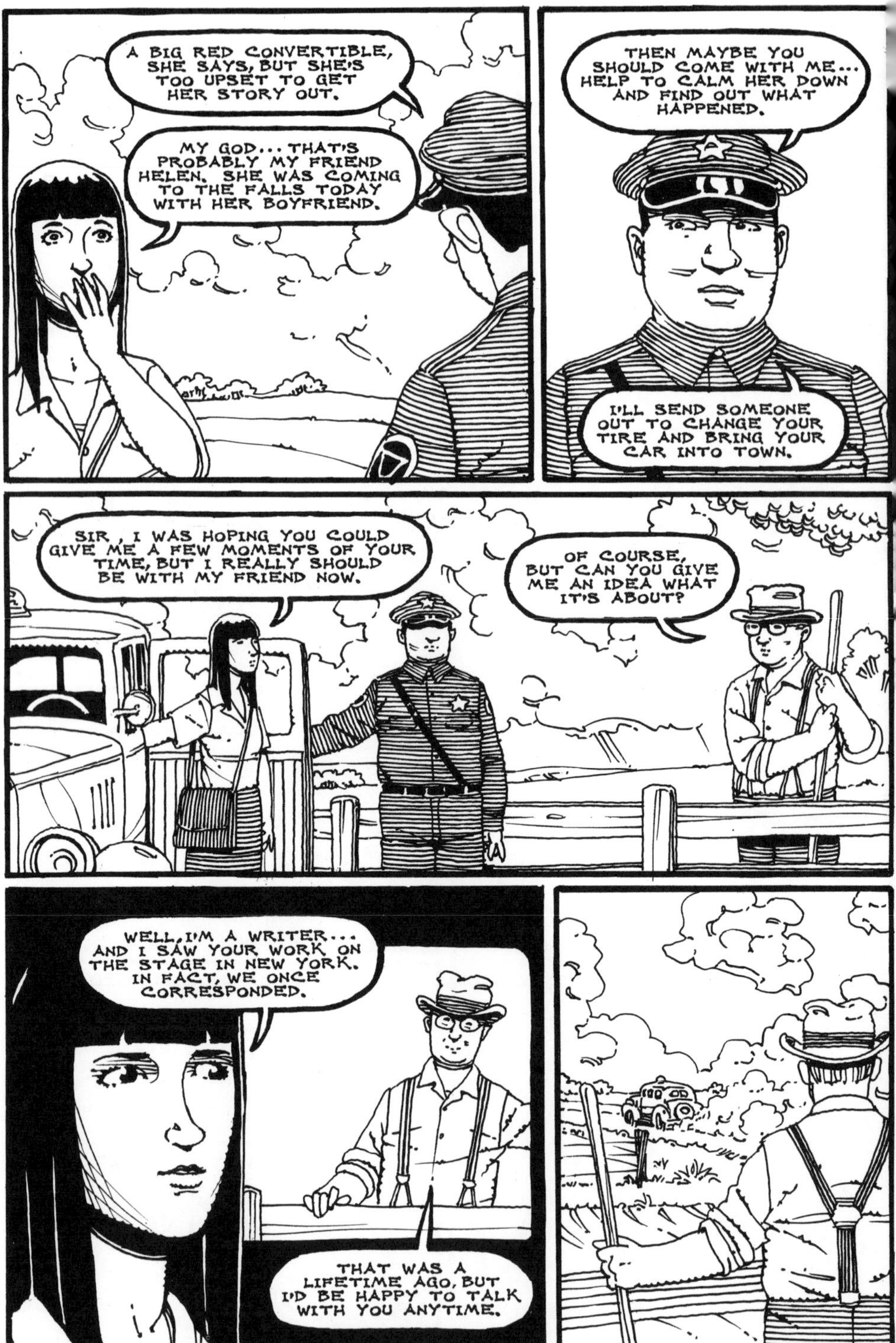

A BIG RED CONVERTIBLE, SHE SAYS, BUT SHE'S TOO UPSET TO GET HER STORY OUT.
MY GOD... THAT'S PROBABLY MY FRIEND HELEN. SHE WAS COMING TO THE FALLS TODAY WITH HER BOYFRIEND.
THEN MAYBE YOU SHOULD COME WITH ME... HELP TO CALM HER DOWN AND FIND OUT WHAT HAPPENED.
I'LL SEND SOMEONE OUT TO CHANGE YOUR TIRE AND BRING YOUR CAR INTO TOWN.
SIR, I WAS HOPING YOU COULD GIVE ME A FEW MOMENTS OF YOUR TIME, BUT I REALLY SHOULD BE WITH MY FRIEND NOW.
OF COURSE, BUT CAN YOU GIVE ME AN IDEA WHAT IT'S ABOUT?
WELL, I'M A WRITER... AND I SAW YOUR WORK ON THE STAGE IN NEW YORK. IN FACT, WE ONCE CORRESPONDED.
THAT WAS A LIFETIME AGO, BUT I'D BE HAPPY TO TALK WITH YOU ANYTIME.

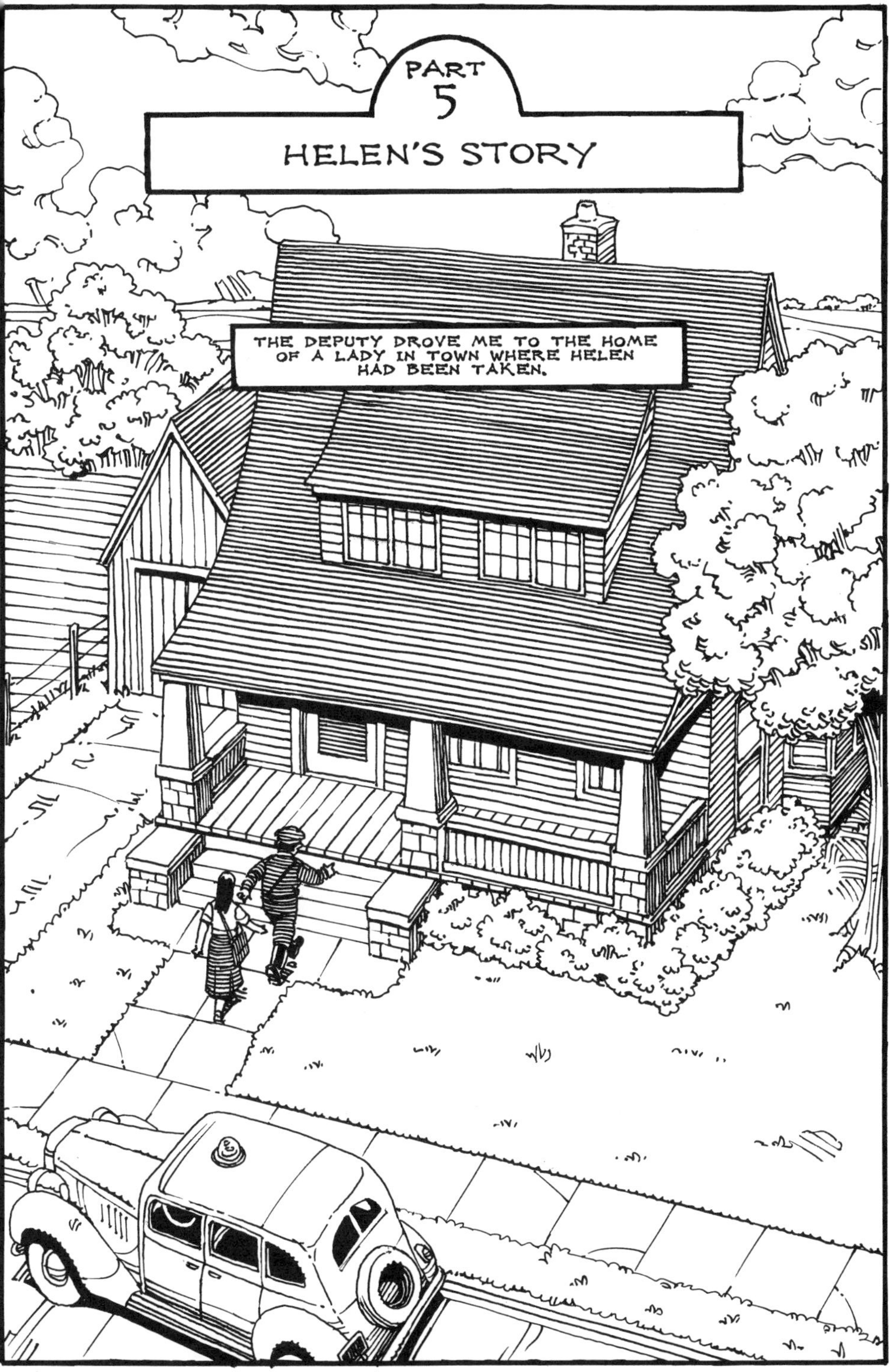
PART
5
HELEN'S STORY
THE DEPUTY DROVE ME TO THE HOME OF A LADY IN TOWN WHERE HELEN HAD BEEN TAKEN.

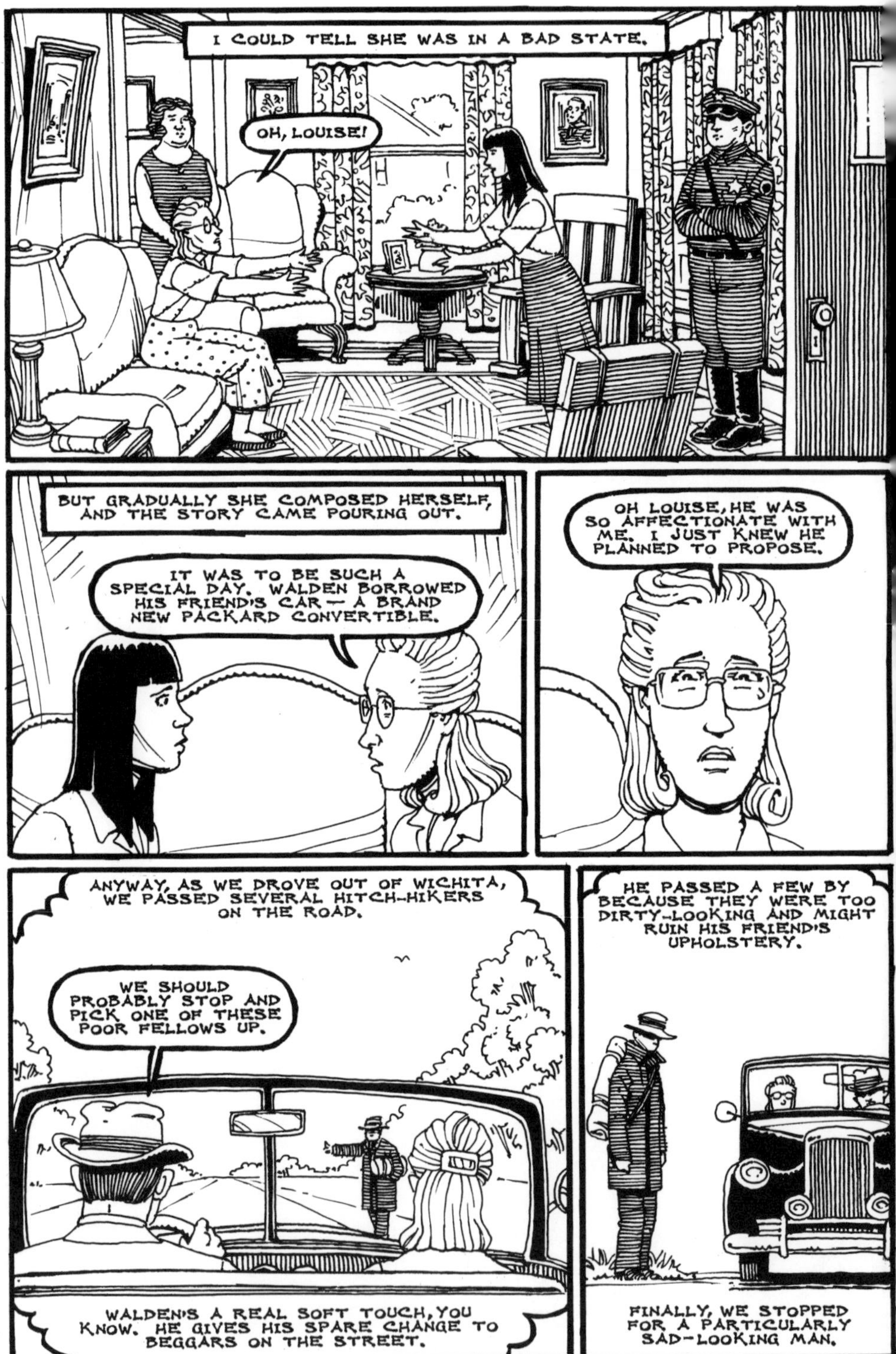
I COULD TELL SHE WAS IN A BAD STATE.
OH, LOUISE!
BUT GRADUALLY SHE COMPOSED HERSELF, AND THE STORY CAME POURING OUT.
IT WAS TO BE SUCH A SPECIAL DAY. WALDEN BORROWED HIS FRIEND'S CAR — A BRAND NEW PACKARD CONVERTIBLE.
OH LOUISE, HE WAS SO AFFECTIONATE WITH ME. I JUST KNEW HE PLANNED TO PROPOSE.
ANYWAY, AS WE DROVE OUT OF WICHITA, WE PASSED SEVERAL HITCH-HIKERS ON THE ROAD.
WE SHOULD PROBABLY STOP AND PICK ONE OF THESE POOR FELLOWS UP.
WALDEN'S A REAL SOFT TOUCH, YOU KNOW. HE GIVES HIS SPARE CHANGE TO BEGGARS ON THE STREET.
HE PASSED A FEW BY BECAUSE THEY WERE TOO DIRTY-LOOKING AND MIGHT RUIN HIS FRIEND'S UPHOLSTERY.
FINALLY, WE STOPPED FOR A PARTICULARLY SAD-LOOKING MAN.

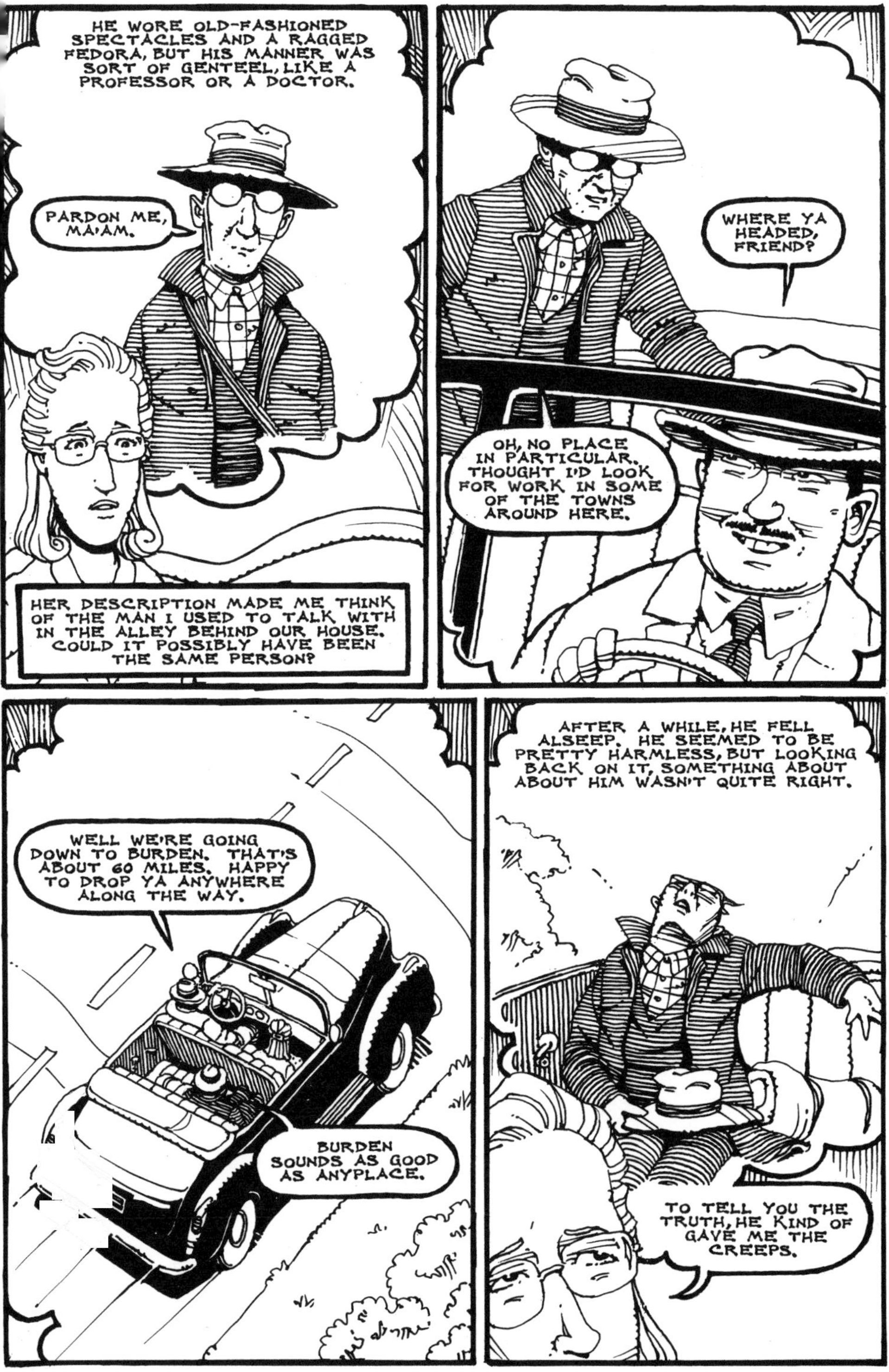
HE WORE OLD-FASHIONED SPECTACLES AND A RAGGED FEDORA, BUT HIS MANNER WAS SORT OF GENTEEL, LIKE A PROFESSOR OR A DOCTOR.
PARDON ME, MA'AM.
HER DESCRIPTION MADE ME THINK OF THE MAN I USED TO TALK WITH IN THE ALLEY BEHIND OUR HOUSE. COULD IT POSSIBLY HAVE BEEN THE SAME PERSON?
WHERE YA HEADED, FRIEND?
OH, NO PLACE IN PARTICULAR. THOUGHT I'D LOOK FOR WORK IN SOME OF THE TOWNS AROUND HERE.
WELL WE'RE GOING DOWN TO BURDEN. THAT'S ABOUT 60 MILES. HAPPY TO DROP YA ANYWHERE ALONG THE WAY.
BURDEN SOUNDS AS GOOD AS ANYPLACE.
AFTER A WHILE, HE FELL ALSEEP. HE SEEMED TO BE PRETTY HARMLESS, BUT LOOKING BACK ON IT, SOMETHING ABOUT ABOUT HIM WASN'T QUITE RIGHT.
TO TELL YOU THE TRUTH, HE KIND OF GAVE ME THE CREEPS.

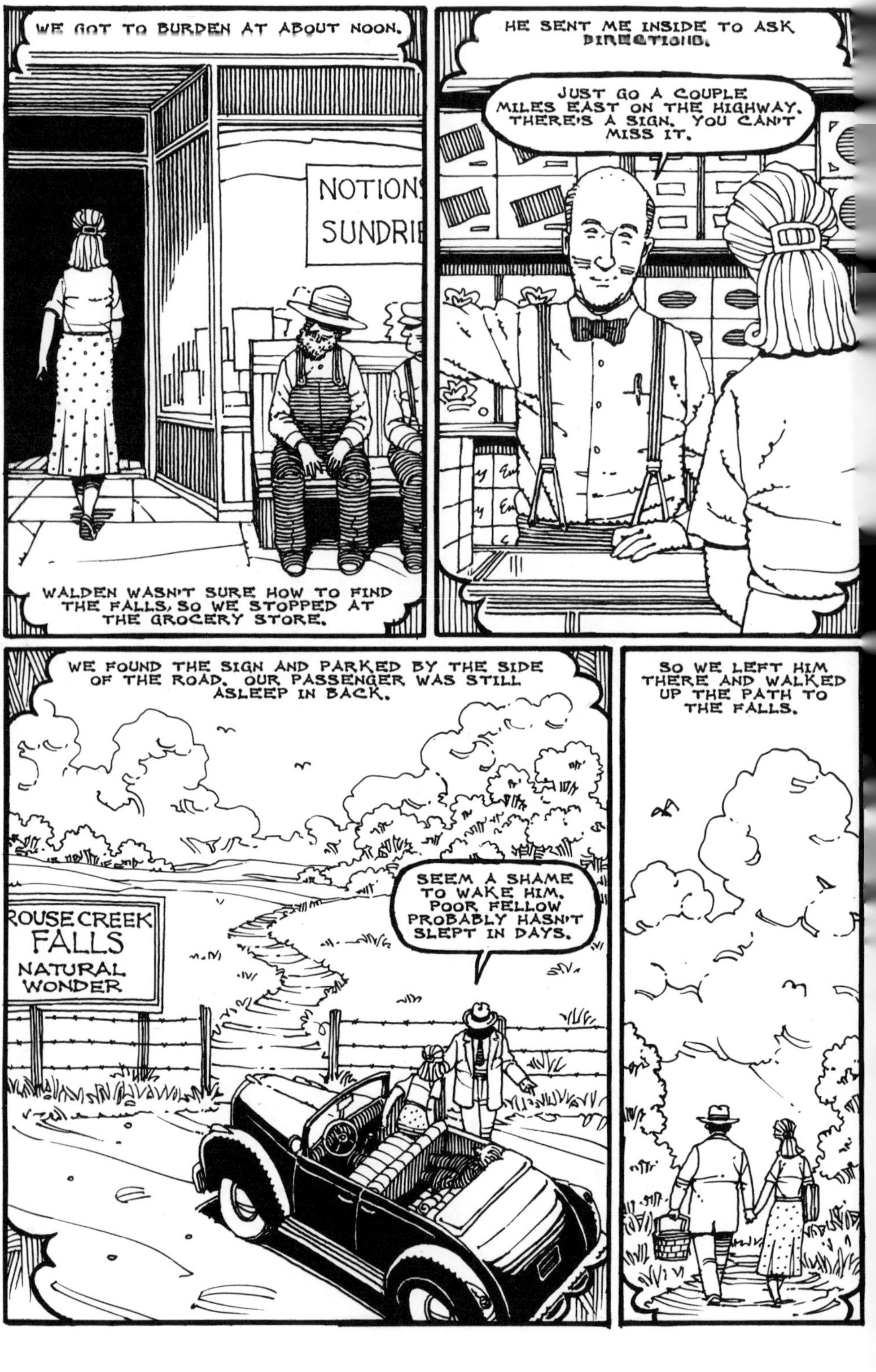
WE GOT TO BURDEN AT ABOUT NOON.
NOTIONS
SUNDRIE
WALDEN WASN'T SURE HOW TO FIND THE FALLS, SO WE STOPPED AT THE GROCERY STORE.
HE SENT ME INSIDE TO ASK DIRECTIONS.
JUST GO A COUPLE MILES EAST ON THE HIGHWAY. THERE'S A SIGN. YOU CAN'T MISS IT.
WE FOUND THE SIGN AND PARKED BY THE SIDE OF THE ROAD. OUR PASSENGER WAS STILL ASLEEP IN BACK.
ROUSE CREEK FALLS NATURAL WONDER
SEEM A SHAME TO WAKE HIM. POOR FELLOW PROBABLY HASN'T SLEPT IN DAYS.
SO WE LEFT HIM THERE AND WALKED UP THE PATH TO THE FALLS.

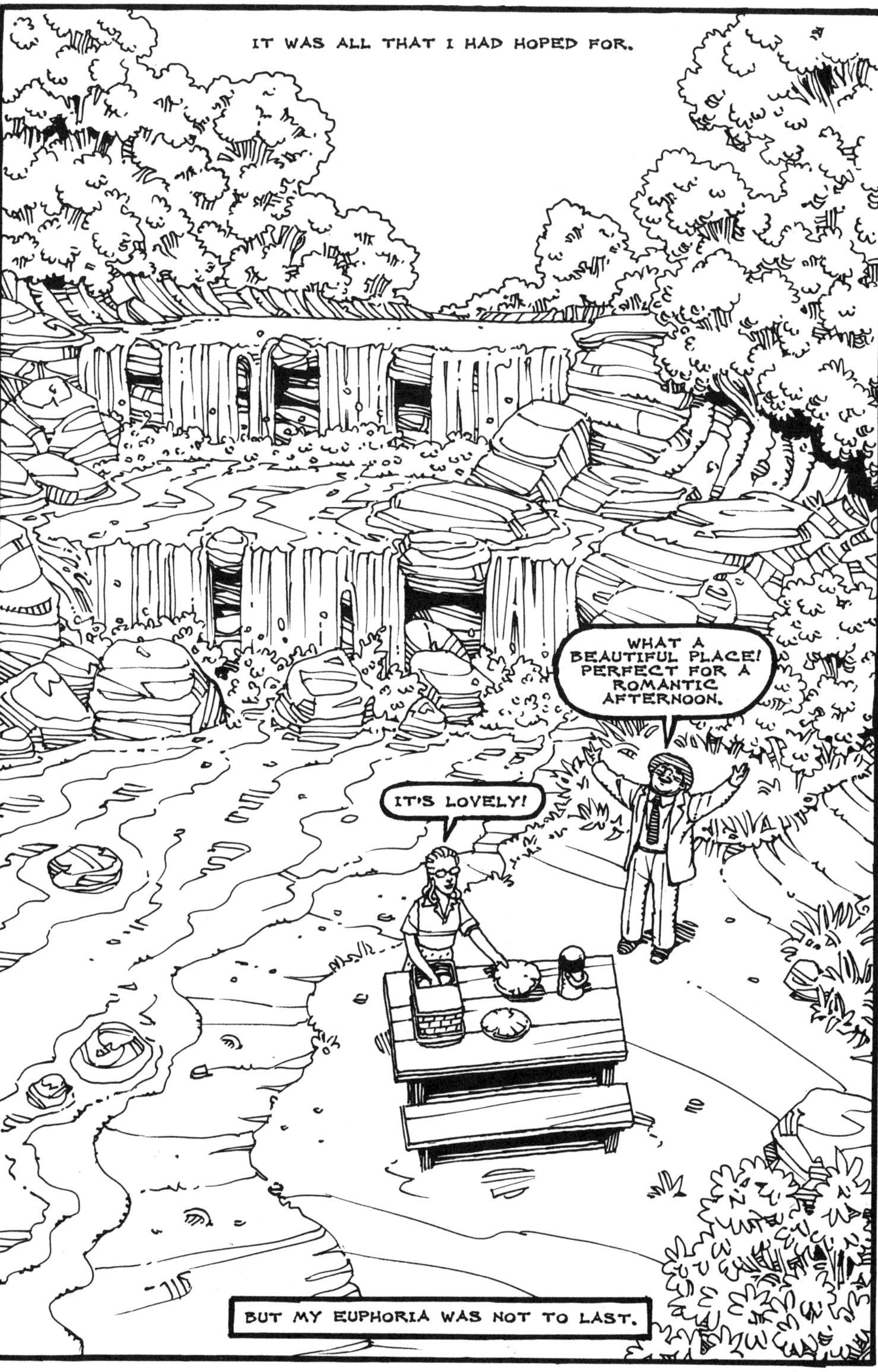
IT WAS ALL THAT I HAD HOPED FOR.
WHAT A BEAUTIFUL PLACE! PERFECT FOR A ROMANTIC AFTERNOON.
IT'S LOVELY!
BUT MY EUPHORIA WAS NOT TO LAST.

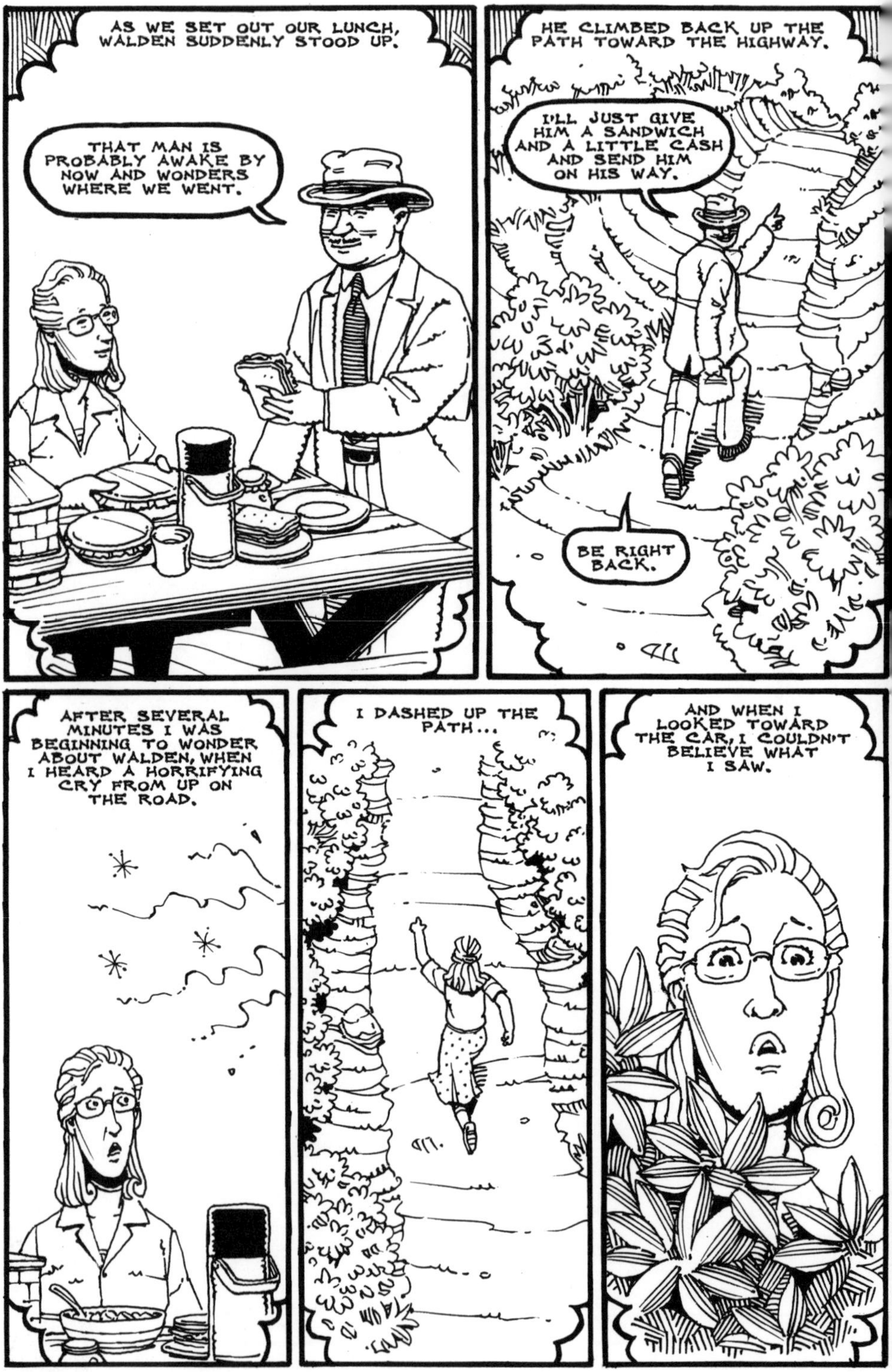
AS WE SET OUT OUR LUNCH, WALDEN SUDDENLY STOOD UP.
THAT MAN IS PROBABLY AWAKE BY NOW AND WONDERS WHERE WE WENT.
HE CLIMBED BACK UP THE PATH TOWARD THE HIGHWAY.
I'LL JUST GIVE HIM A SANDWICH AND A LITTLE CASH AND SEND HIM ON HIS WAY.
BE RIGHT BACK.
AFTER SEVERAL MINUTES I WAS BEGINNING TO WONDER ABOUT WALDEN, WHEN I HEARD A HORRIFYING CRY FROM UP ON THE ROAD.
I DASHED UP THE PATH...
AND WHEN I LOOKED TOWARD THE CAR, I COULDN'T BELIEVE WHAT I SAW.

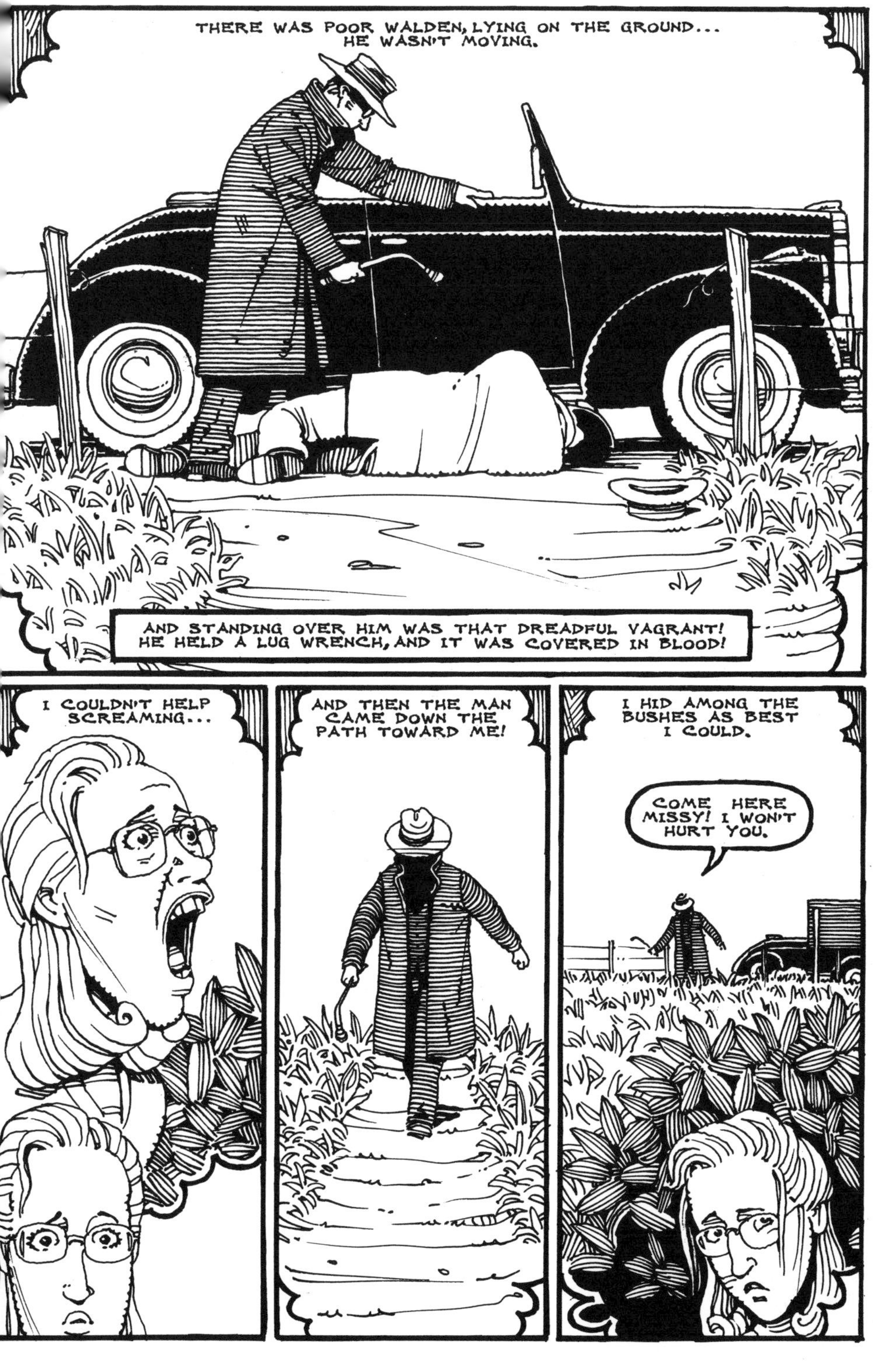

THERE WAS POOR WALDEN, LYING ON THE GROUND... HE WASN'T MOVING.
AND STANDING OVER HIM WAS THAT DREADFUL VAGRANT! HE HELD A LUG WRENCH, AND IT WAS COVERED IN BLOOD!
I COULDN'T HELP SCREAMING...
AND THEN THE MAN CAME DOWN THE PATH TOWARD ME!
I HID AMONG THE BUSHES AS BEST I COULD.
COME HERE MISSY! I WON'T HURT YOU.

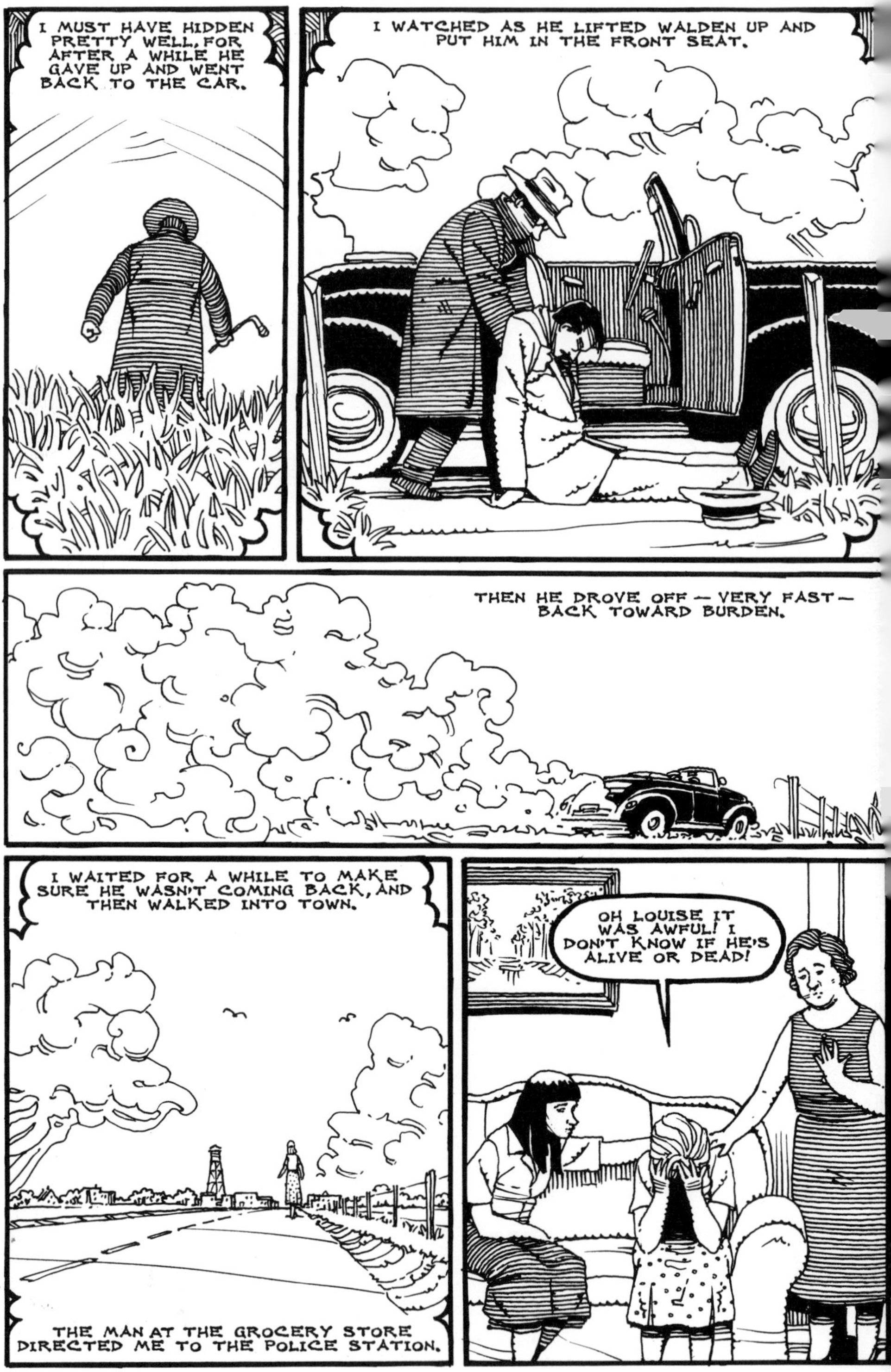
I MUST HAVE HIDDEN PRETTY WELL, FOR AFTER A WHILE HE GAVE UP AND WENT BACK TO THE CAR.
I WATCHED AS HE LIFTED WALDEN UP AND PUT HIM IN THE FRONT SEAT.
THEN HE DROVE OFF — VERY FAST — BACK TOWARD BURDEN.
I WAITED FOR A WHILE TO MAKE SURE HE WASN'T COMING BACK, AND THEN WALKED INTO TOWN.
THE MAN AT THE GROCERY STORE DIRECTED ME TO THE POLICE STATION.
OH LOUISE IT WAS AWFUL! I DON'T KNOW IF HE'S ALIVE OR DEAD!

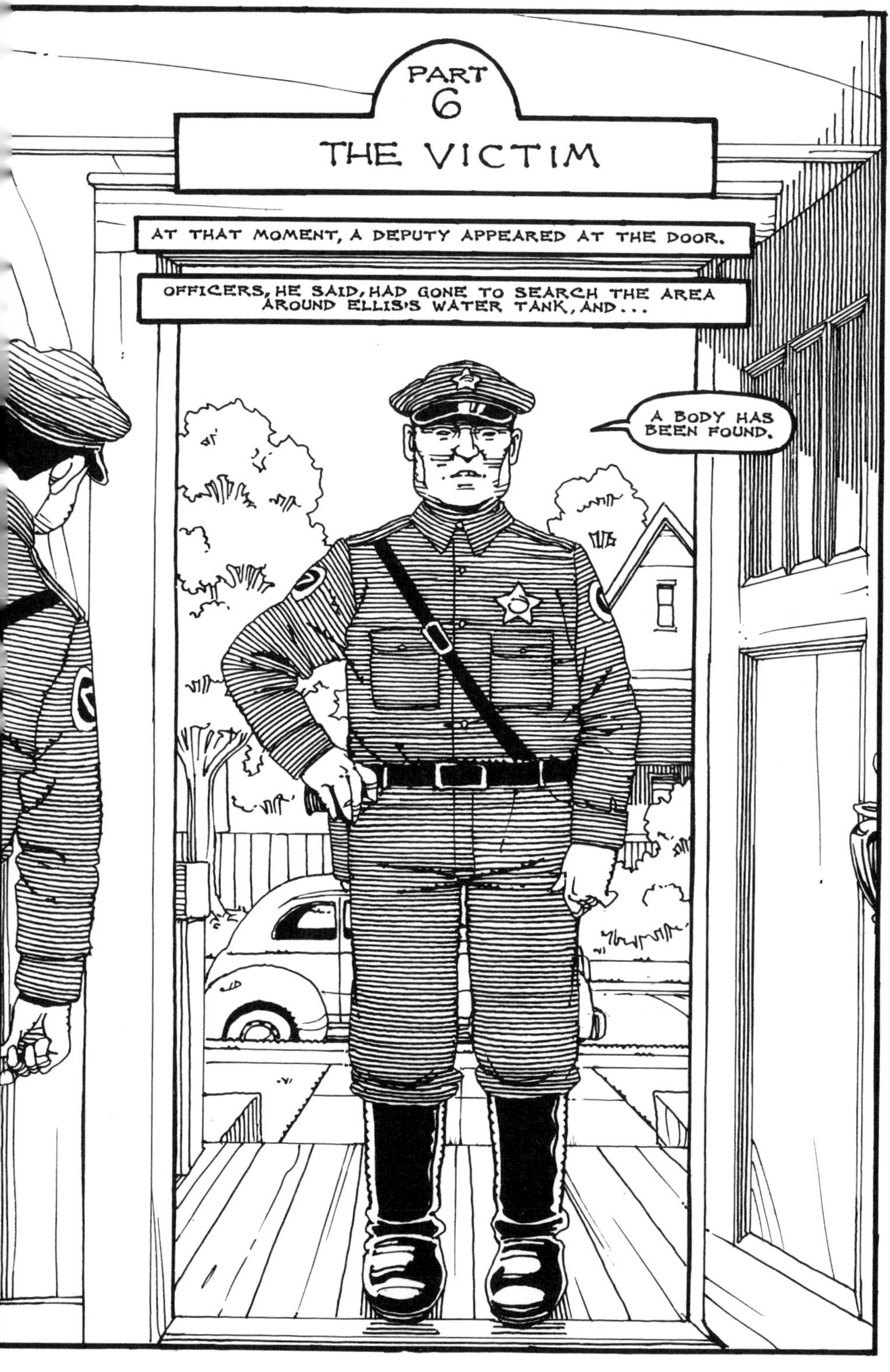
PART 6
THE VICTIM
AT THAT MOMENT, A DEPUTY APPEARED AT THE DOOR.
OFFICERS, HE SAID, HAD GONE TO SEARCH THE AREA AROUND ELLIS'S WATER TANK, AND...
A BODY HAS BEEN FOUND.

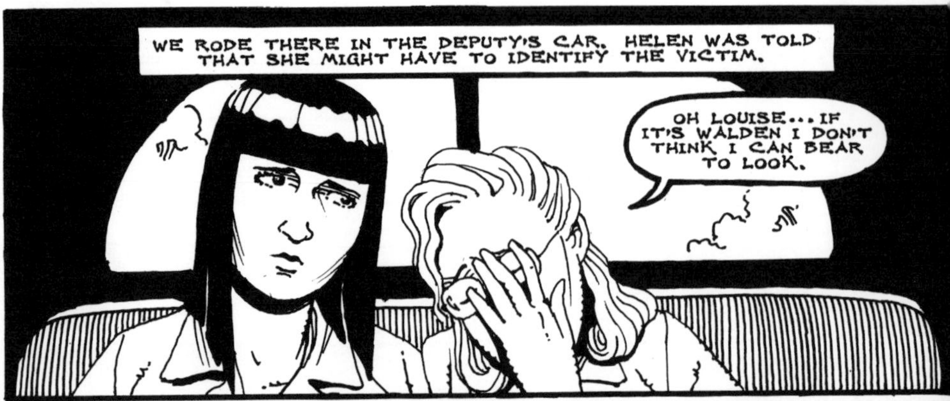
WE RODE THERE IN THE DEPUTY'S CAR. HELEN WAS TOLD THAT SHE MIGHT HAVE TO IDENTIFY THE VICTIM.
OH LOUISE... IF IT'S WALDEN I DON'T THINK I CAN BEAR TO LOOK.

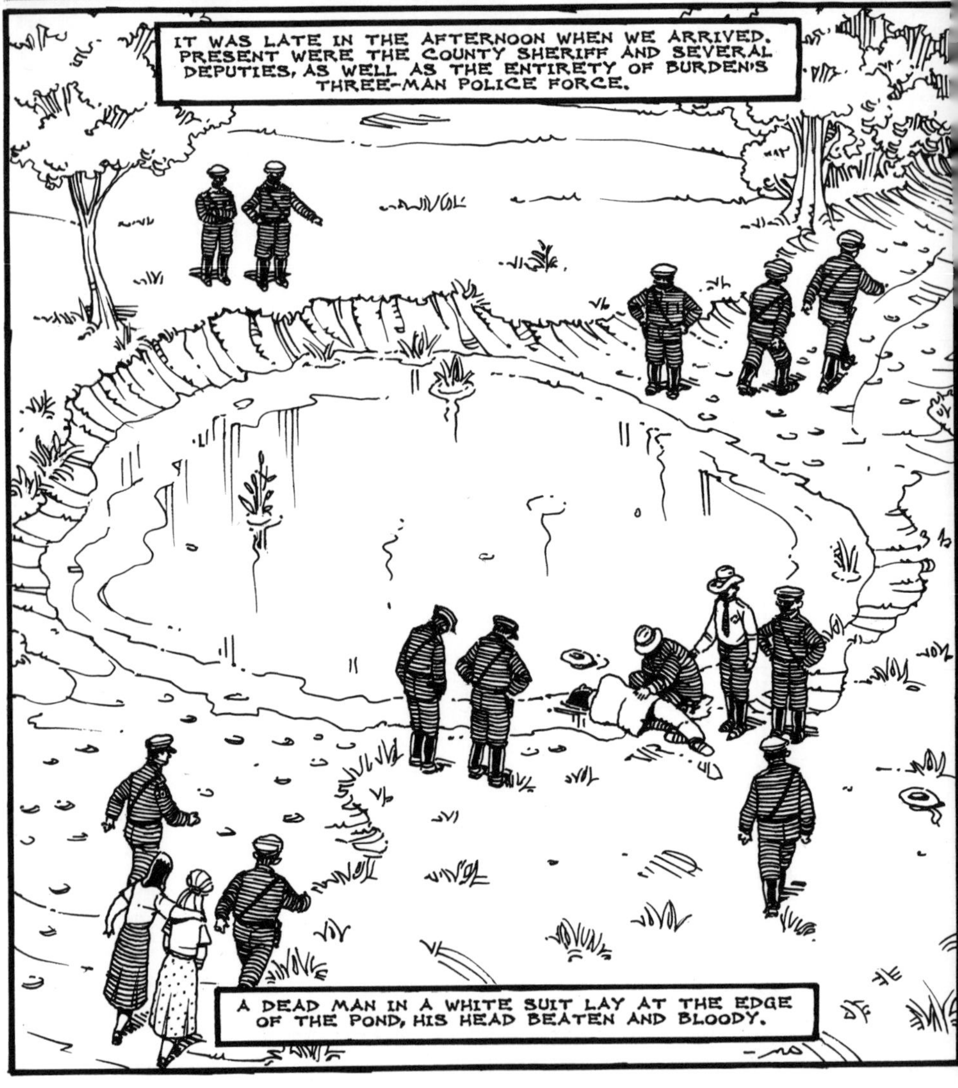
IT WAS LATE IN THE AFTERNOON WHEN WE ARRIVED. PRESENT WERE THE COUNTY SHERIFF AND SEVERAL DEPUTIES, AS WELL AS THE ENTIRETY OF BURDEN'S THREE-MAN POLICE FORCE.
A DEAD MAN IN A WHITE SUIT LAY AT THE EDGE OF THE POND, HIS HEAD BEATEN AND BLOODY.

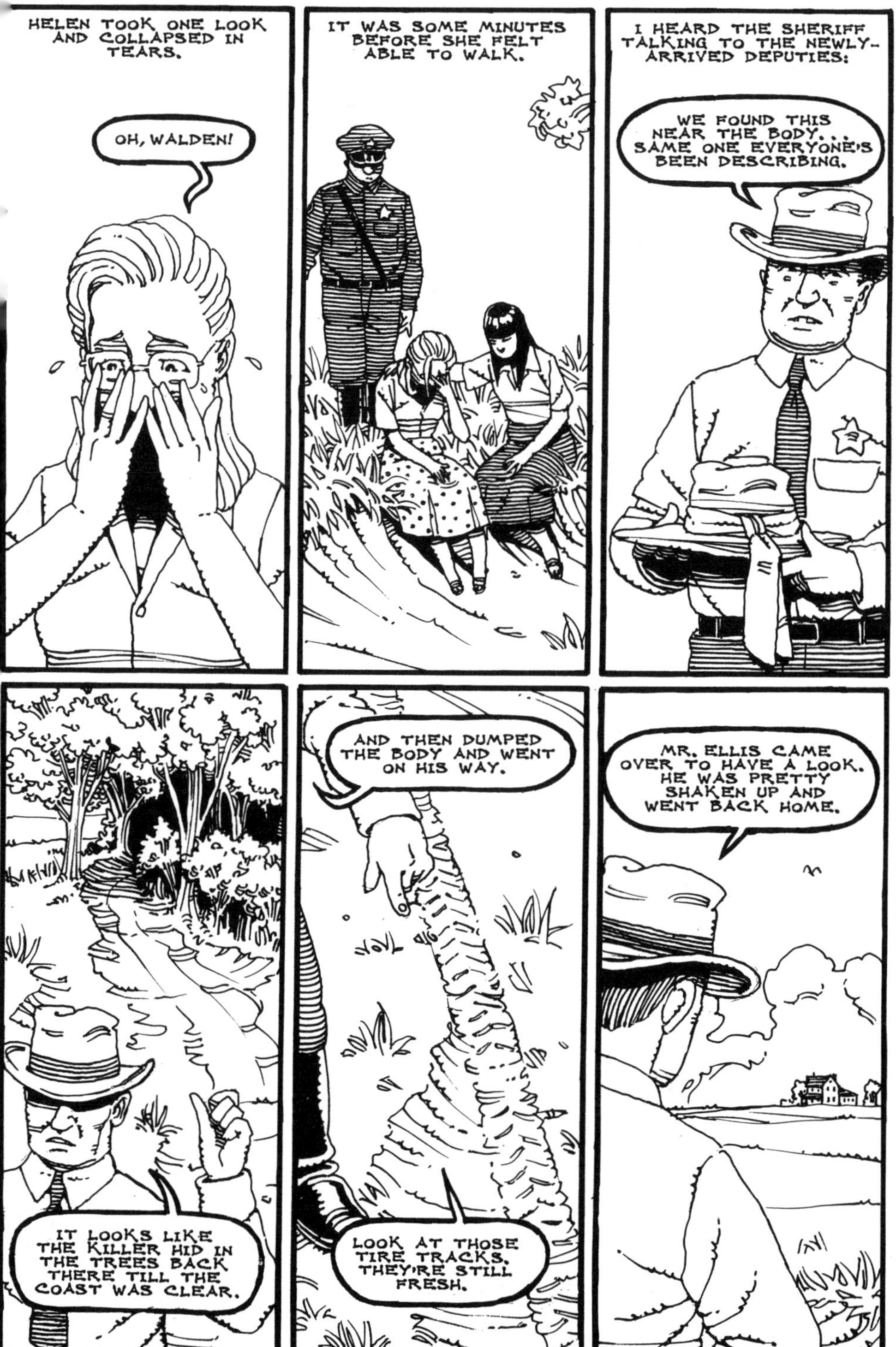
HELEN TOOK ONE LOOK AND COLLAPSED IN TEARS.
OH, WALDEN!
IT WAS SOME MINUTES BEFORE SHE FELT ABLE TO WALK.
I HEARD THE SHERIFF TALKING TO THE NEWLY-ARRIVED DEPUTIES:
WE FOUND THIS NEAR THE BODY... SAME ONE EVERYONE'S BEEN DESCRIBING.
IT LOOKS LIKE THE KILLER HID IN THE TREES BACK THERE TILL THE COAST WAS CLEAR.
AND THEN DUMPED THE BODY AND WENT ON HIS WAY.
LOOK AT THOSE TIRE TRACKS. THEY'RE STILL FRESH.
MR. ELLIS CAME OVER TO HAVE A LOOK. HE WAS PRETTY SHAKEN UP AND WENT BACK HOME.

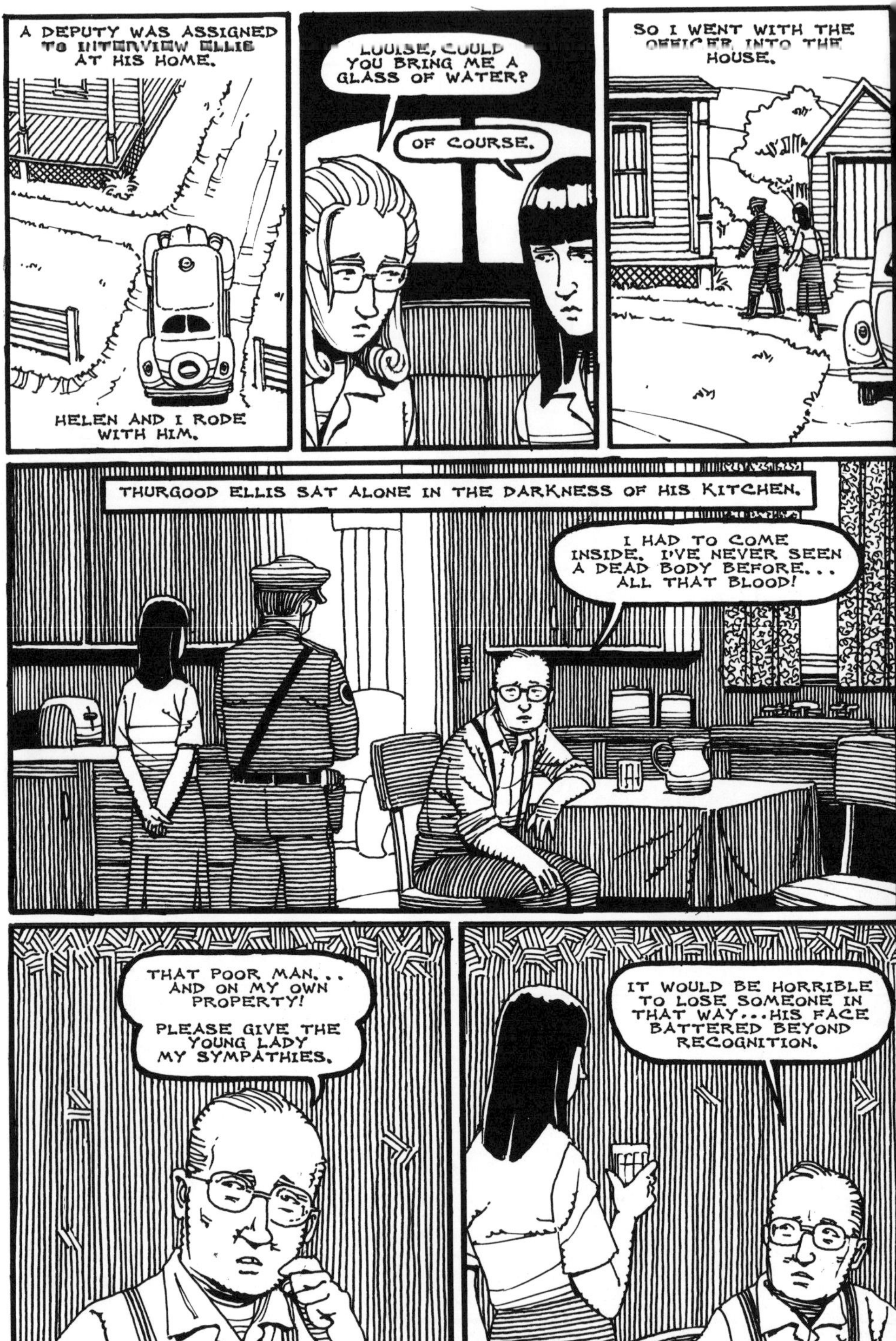
A DEPUTY WAS ASSIGNED TO INTERVIEW ELLIS AT HIS HOME.
HELEN AND I RODE WITH HIM.
LOUISE, COULD YOU BRING ME A GLASS OF WATER?
OF COURSE.
SO I WENT WITH THE OFFICER INTO THE HOUSE.
THURGOOD ELLIS SAT ALONE IN THE DARKNESS OF HIS KITCHEN.
I HAD TO COME INSIDE. I'VE NEVER SEEN A DEAD BODY BEFORE... ALL THAT BLOOD!
THAT POOR MAN... AND ON MY OWN PROPERTY!
PLEASE GIVE THE YOUNG LADY MY SYMPATHIES.
IT WOULD BE HORRIBLE TO LOSE SOMEONE IN THAT WAY...HIS FACE BATTERED BEYOND RECOGNITION.

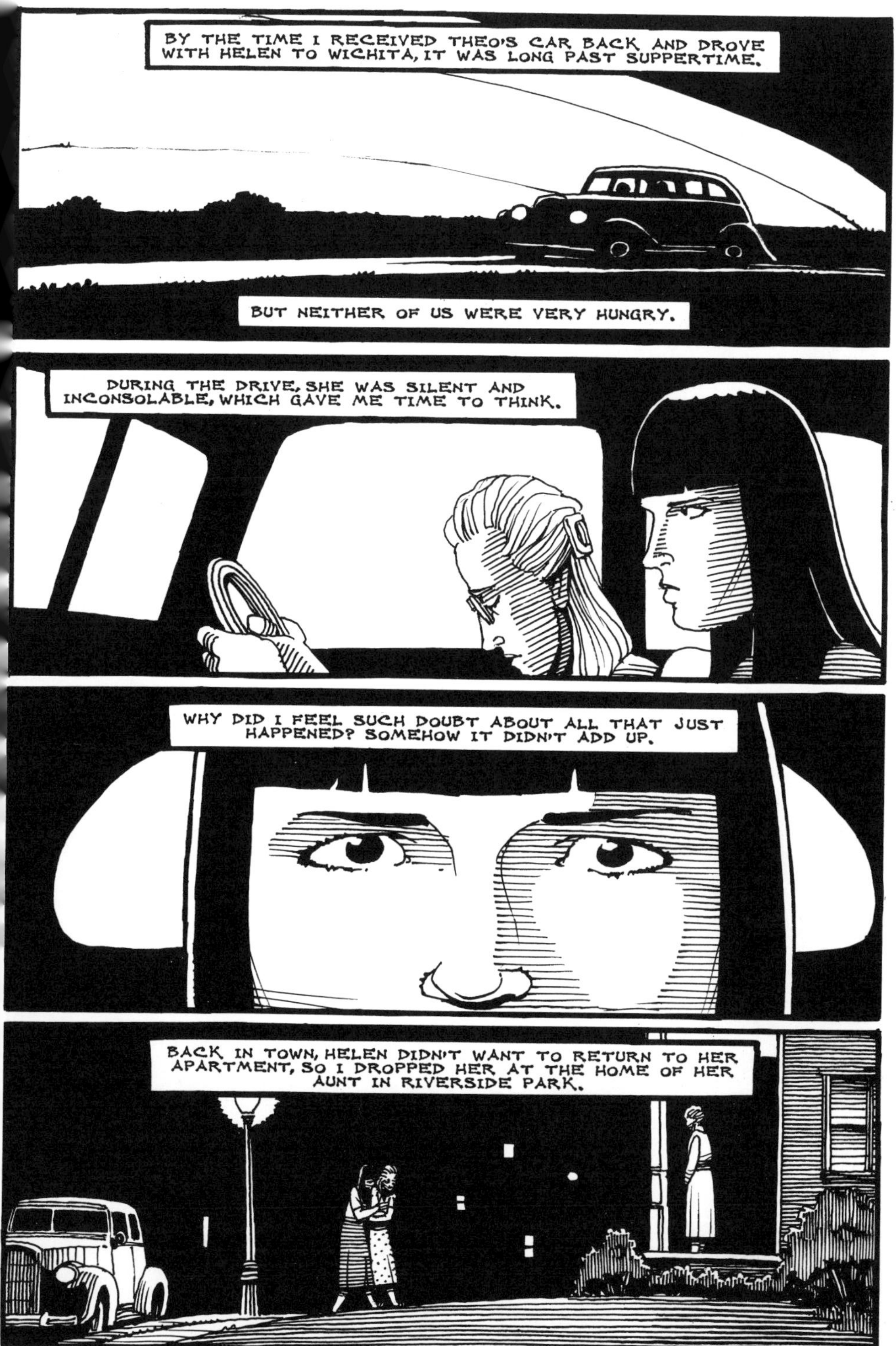
BY THE TIME I RECEIVED THEO'S CAR BACK AND DROVE WITH HELEN TO WICHITA, IT WAS LONG PAST SUPPERTIME.
BUT NEITHER OF US WERE VERY HUNGRY.
DURING THE DRIVE, SHE WAS SILENT AND INCONSOLABLE, WHICH GAVE ME TIME TO THINK.
WHY DID I FEEL SUCH DOUBT ABOUT ALL THAT JUST HAPPENED? SOMEHOW IT DIDN'T ADD UP.
BACK IN TOWN, HELEN DIDN'T WANT TO RETURN TO HER APARTMENT, SO I DROPPED HER AT THE HOME OF HER AUNT IN RIVERSIDE PARK.

BACK AT HOME, I STAYED UP INTO THE NIGHT.

I SEARCHED THROUGH MY OLD PAPERS UNTIL I FOUND IT: THE SINGLE LETTER I HAD RECEIVED YEARS EARLIER FROM THURGOOD ELLIS...

THE CELEBRATED GENIUS DEIGNING TO COMMUNICATE WITH AN UNKNOWN AND OPINIONATED YOUNG DANCER.

IN THE EARLY HOURS OF SUNDAY MORNING, I THOUGHT I HAD THE MYSTERY UNTANGLED...

BUT I HAD TO BE CERTAIN.

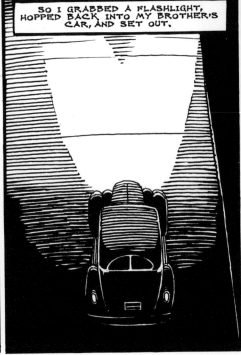

SO I GRABBED A FLASHLIGHT, HOPPED BACK INTO MY BROTHER'S CAR, AND SET OUT.

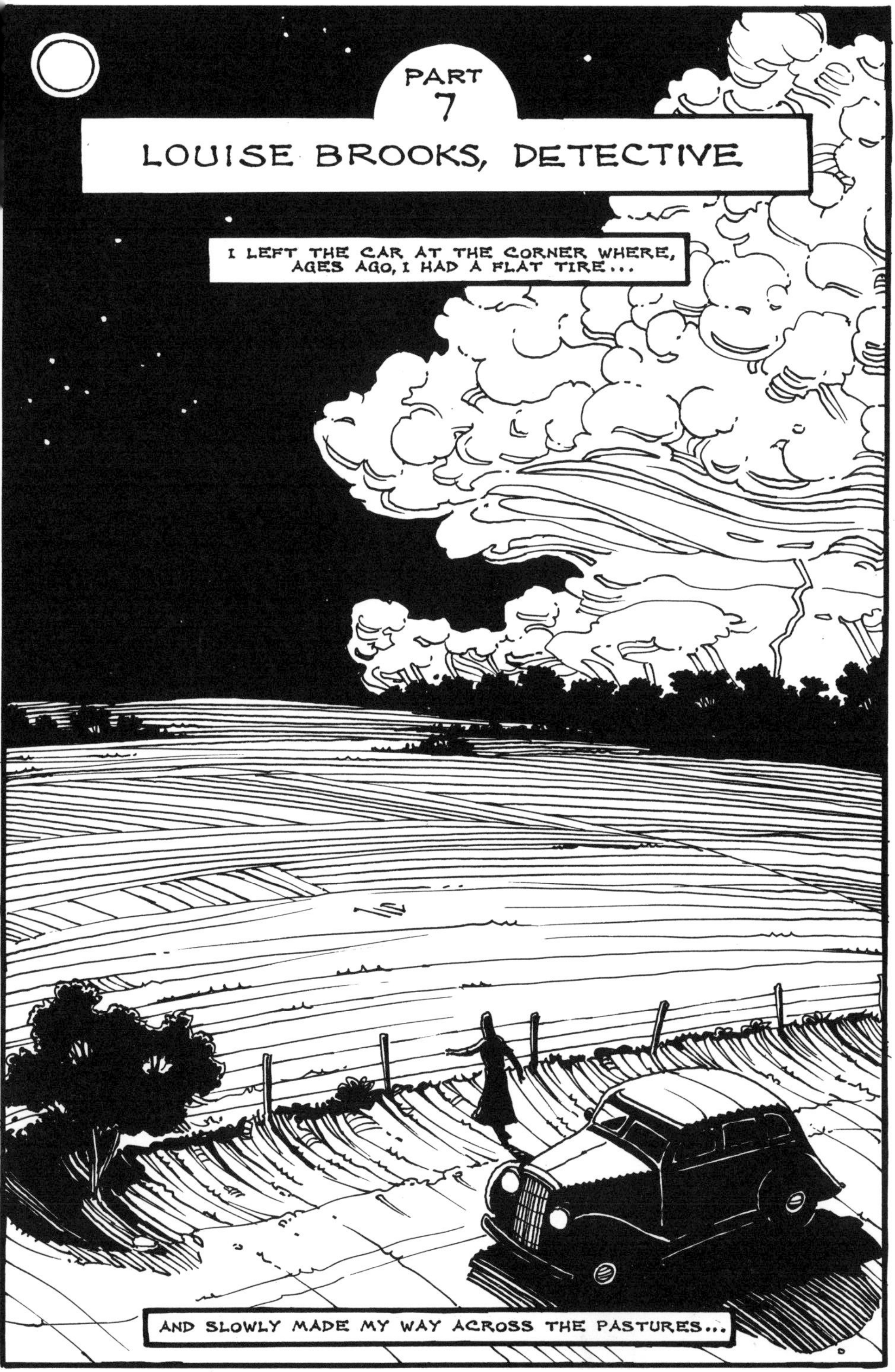
PART 7
LOUISE BROOKS, DETECTIVE
I LEFT THE CAR AT THE CORNER WHERE, AGES AGO, I HAD A FLAT TIRE...
AND SLOWLY MADE MY WAY ACROSS THE PASTURES...

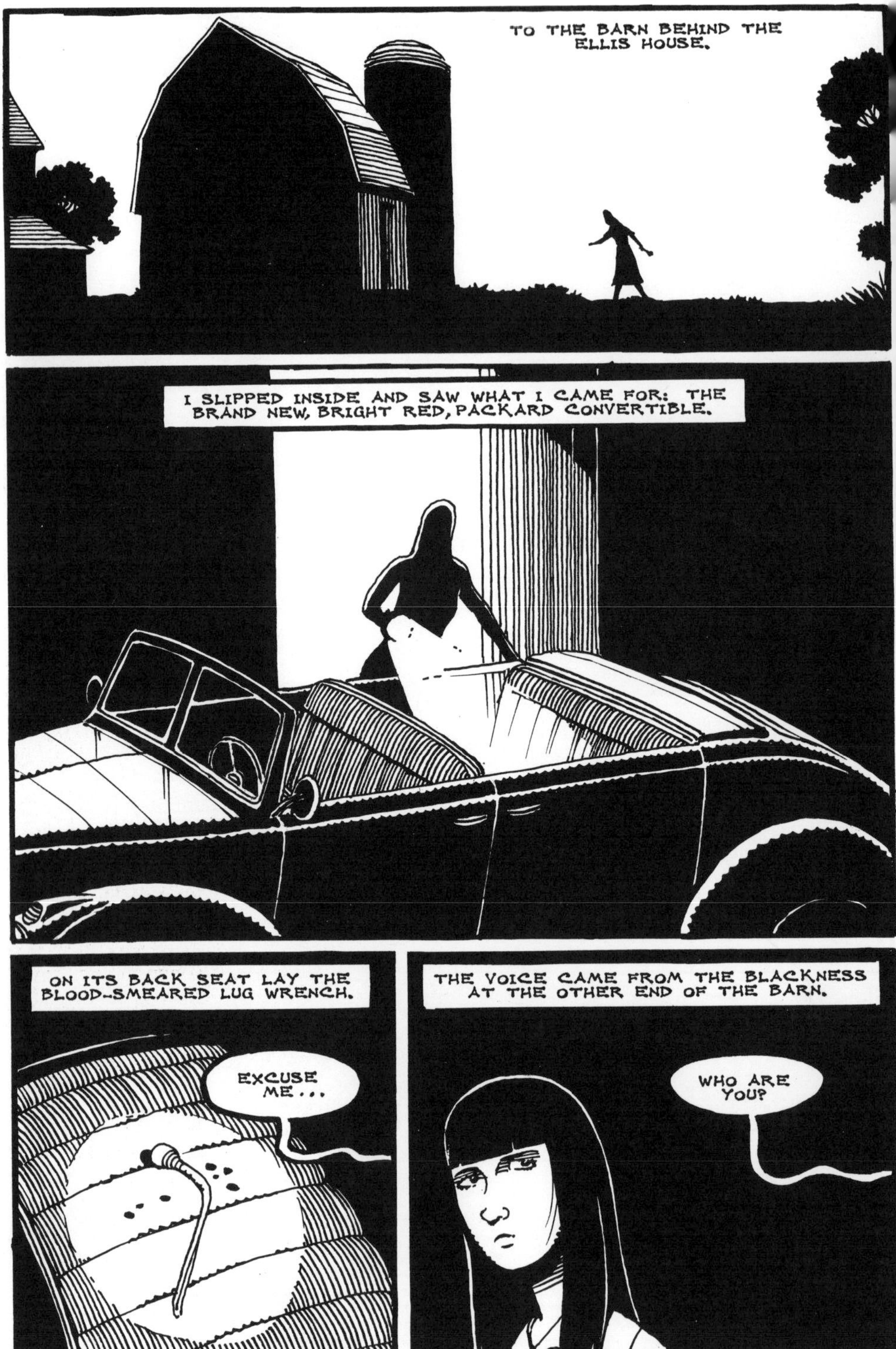
TO THE BARN BEHIND THE ELLIS HOUSE.
I SLIPPED INSIDE AND SAW WHAT I CAME FOR: THE BRAND NEW, BRIGHT RED, PACKARD CONVERTIBLE.
ON ITS BACK SEAT LAY THE BLOOD-SMEARED LUG WRENCH.
EXCUSE ME...
THE VOICE CAME FROM THE BLACKNESS AT THE OTHER END OF THE BARN.
WHO ARE YOU?

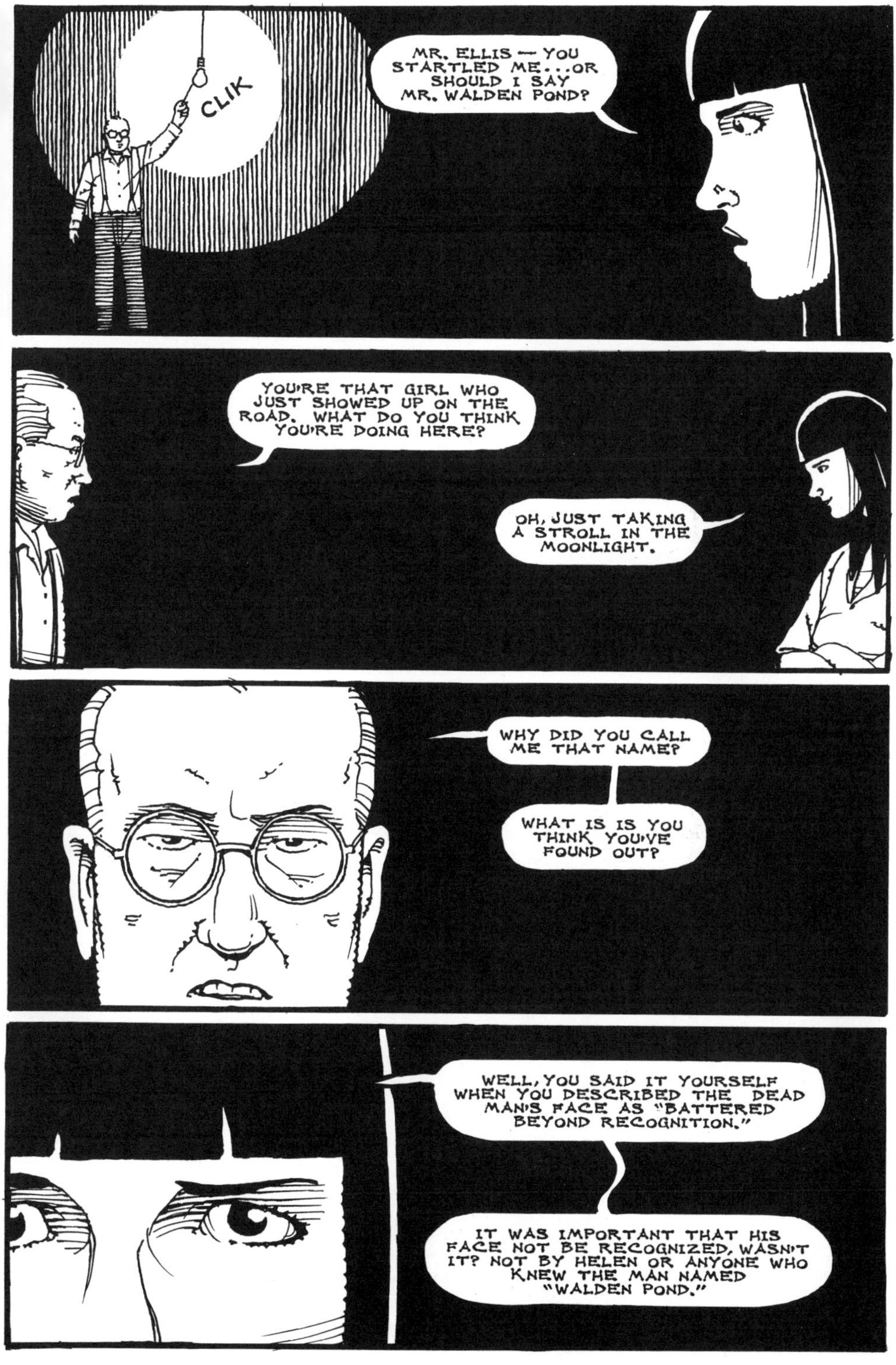
CLIK
MR. ELLIS — YOU STARTLED ME...OR SHOULD I SAY MR. WALDEN POND?
YOU'RE THAT GIRL WHO JUST SHOWED UP ON THE ROAD. WHAT DO YOU THINK YOU'RE DOING HERE?
OH, JUST TAKING A STROLL IN THE MOONLIGHT.
WHY DID YOU CALL ME THAT NAME?
WHAT IS IS YOU THINK YOU'VE FOUND OUT?
WELL, YOU SAID IT YOURSELF WHEN YOU DESCRIBED THE DEAD MAN'S FACE AS "BATTERED BEYOND RECOGNITION."
IT WAS IMPORTANT THAT HIS FACE NOT BE RECOGNIZED, WASN'T IT? NOT BY HELEN OR ANYONE WHO KNEW THE MAN NAMED "WALDEN POND."

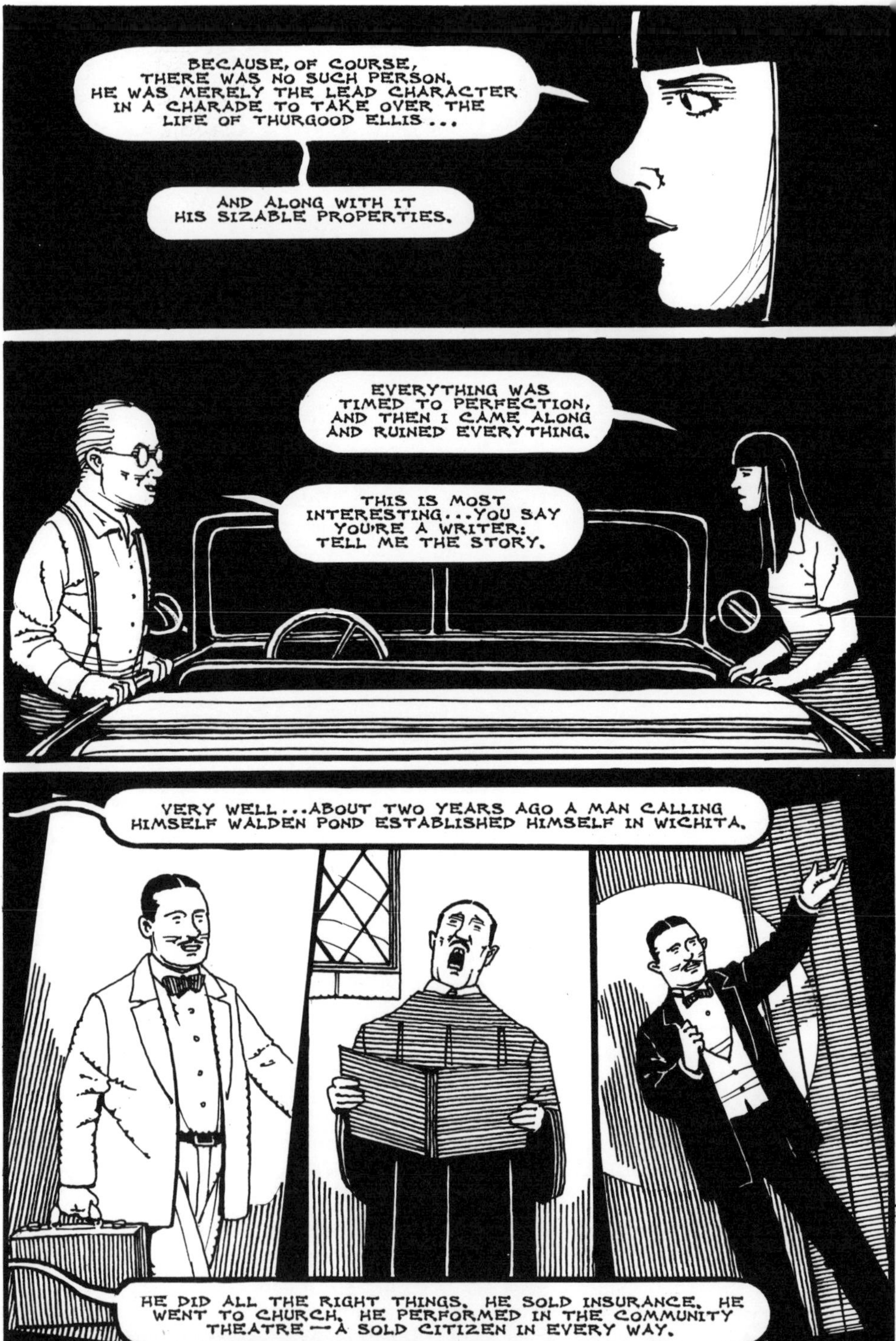
BECAUSE, OF COURSE, THERE WAS NO SUCH PERSON. HE WAS MERELY THE LEAD CHARACTER IN A CHARADE TO TAKE OVER THE LIFE OF THURGOOD ELLIS...
AND ALONG WITH IT HIS SIZABLE PROPERTIES.
EVERYTHING WAS TIMED TO PERFECTION, AND THEN I CAME ALONG AND RUINED EVERYTHING.
THIS IS MOST INTERESTING...YOU SAY YOU'RE A WRITER: TELL ME THE STORY.
VERY WELL...ABOUT TWO YEARS AGO A MAN CALLING HIMSELF WALDEN POND ESTABLISHED HIMSELF IN WICHITA.
HE DID ALL THE RIGHT THINGS. HE SOLD INSURANCE. HE WENT TO CHURCH. HE PERFORMED IN THE COMMUNITY THEATRE—A SOLD CITIZEN IN EVERY WAY.

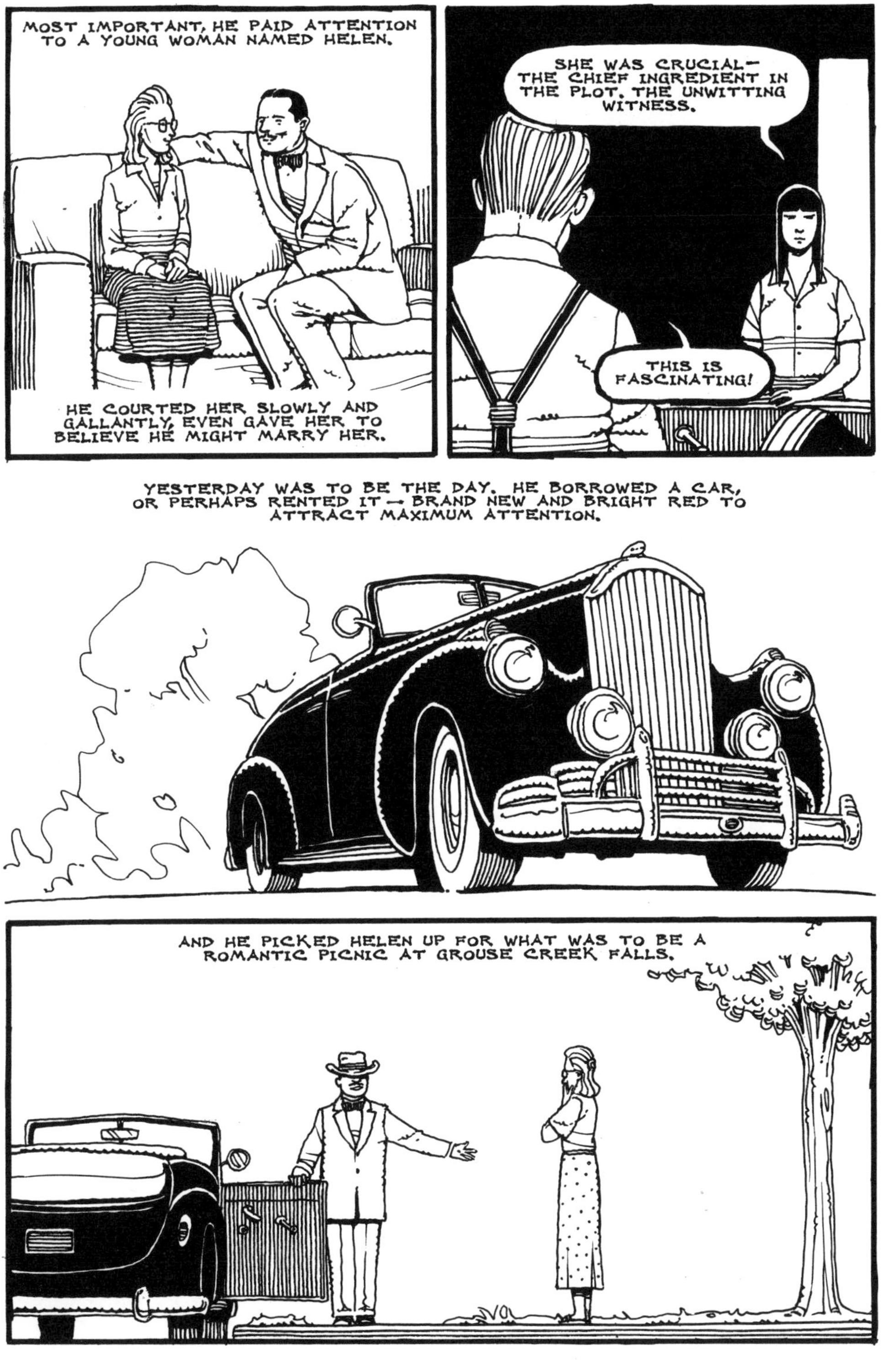
MOST IMPORTANT, HE PAID ATTENTION TO A YOUNG WOMAN NAMED HELEN.
HE COURTED HER SLOWLY AND GALLANTLY, EVEN GAVE HER TO BELIEVE HE MIGHT MARRY HER.
SHE WAS CRUCIAL— THE CHIEF INGREDIENT IN THE PLOT, THE UNWITTING WITNESS.
THIS IS FASCINATING!
YESTERDAY WAS TO BE THE DAY. HE BORROWED A CAR, OR PERHAPS RENTED IT → BRAND NEW AND BRIGHT RED TO ATTRACT MAXIMUM ATTENTION.
AND HE PICKED HELEN UP FOR WHAT WAS TO BE A ROMANTIC PICNIC AT GROUSE CREEK FALLS.

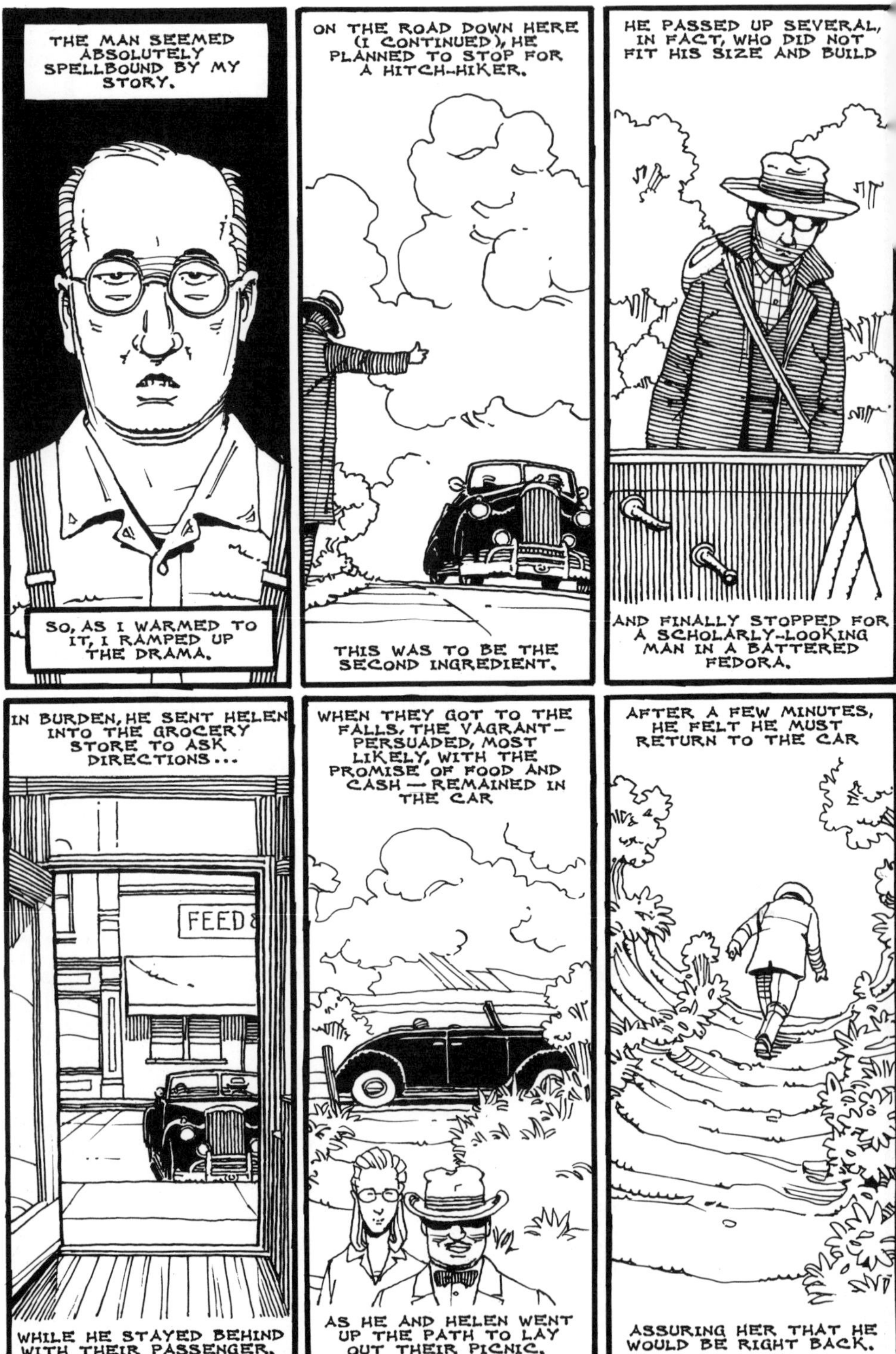
THE MAN SEEMED ABSOLUTELY SPELLBOUND BY MY STORY.
SO, AS I WARMED TO IT, I RAMPED UP THE DRAMA.
ON THE ROAD DOWN HERE (I CONTINUED), HE PLANNED TO STOP FOR A HITCH-HIKER.
THIS WAS TO BE THE SECOND INGREDIENT.
HE PASSED UP SEVERAL, IN FACT, WHO DID NOT FIT HIS SIZE AND BUILD
AND FINALLY STOPPED FOR A SCHOLARLY-LOOKING MAN IN A BATTERED FEDORA.
IN BURDEN, HE SENT HELEN INTO THE GROCERY STORE TO ASK DIRECTIONS...
FEED
WHILE HE STAYED BEHIND WITH THEIR PASSENGER.
WHEN THEY GOT TO THE FALLS, THE VAGRANT—PERSUADED, MOST LIKELY, WITH THE PROMISE OF FOOD AND CASH—REMAINED IN THE CAR
AS HE AND HELEN WENT UP THE PATH TO LAY OUT THEIR PICNIC.
AFTER A FEW MINUTES, HE FELT HE MUST RETURN TO THE CAR
ASSURING HER THAT HE WOULD BE RIGHT BACK.

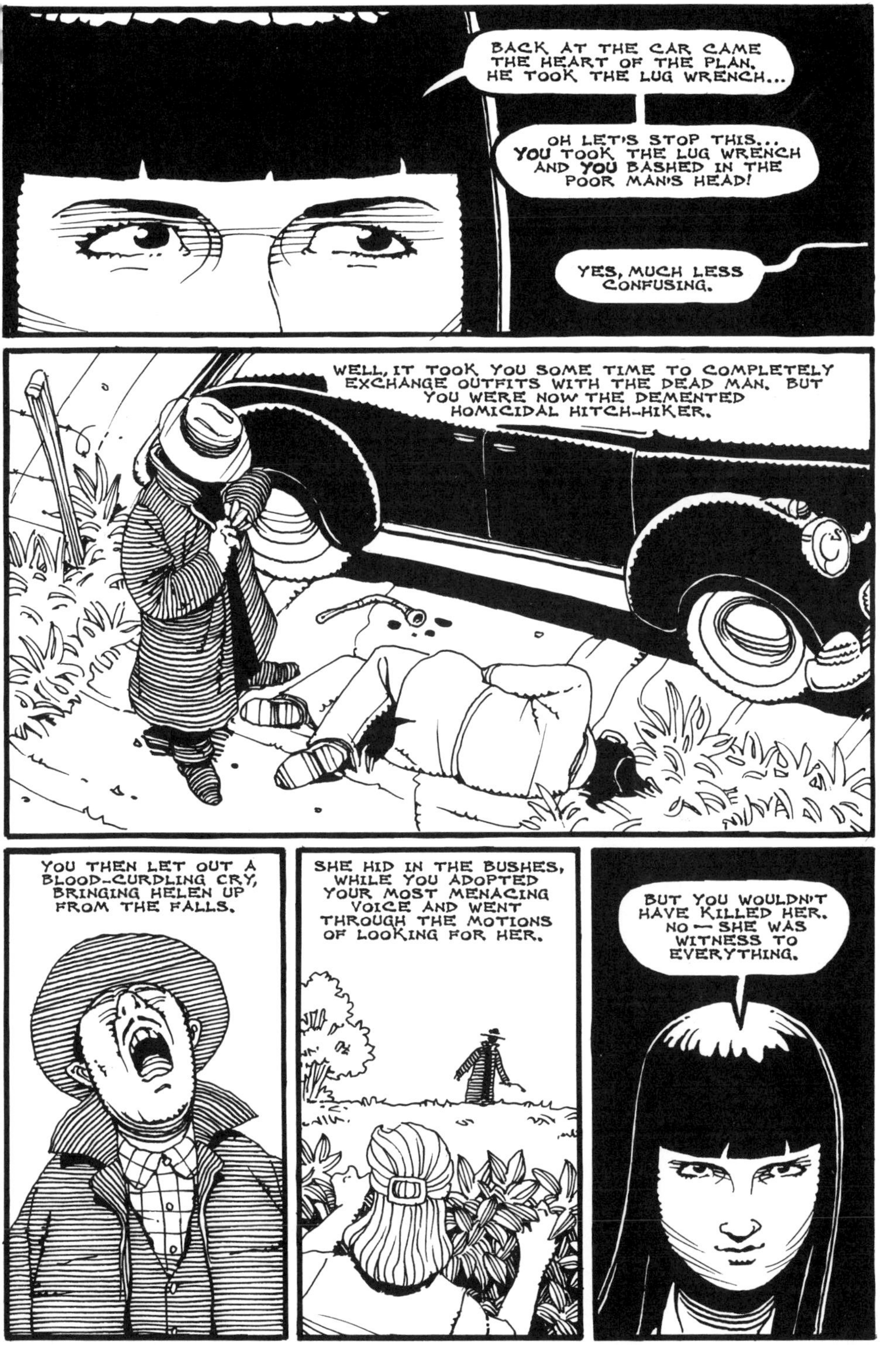
BACK AT THE CAR CAME THE HEART OF THE PLAN. HE TOOK THE LUG WRENCH...
OH LET'S STOP THIS... YOU TOOK THE LUG WRENCH AND YOU BASHED IN THE POOR MAN'S HEAD!
YES, MUCH LESS CONFUSING.
WELL, IT TOOK YOU SOME TIME TO COMPLETELY EXCHANGE OUTFITS WITH THE DEAD MAN. BUT YOU WERE NOW THE DEMENTED HOMICIDAL HITCH-HIKER.
YOU THEN LET OUT A BLOOD-CURDLING CRY, BRINGING HELEN UP FROM THE FALLS.
SHE HID IN THE BUSHES, WHILE YOU ADOPTED YOUR MOST MENACING VOICE AND WENT THROUGH THE MOTIONS OF LOOKING FOR HER.
BUT YOU WOULDN'T HAVE KILLED HER. NO — SHE WAS WITNESS TO EVERYTHING.

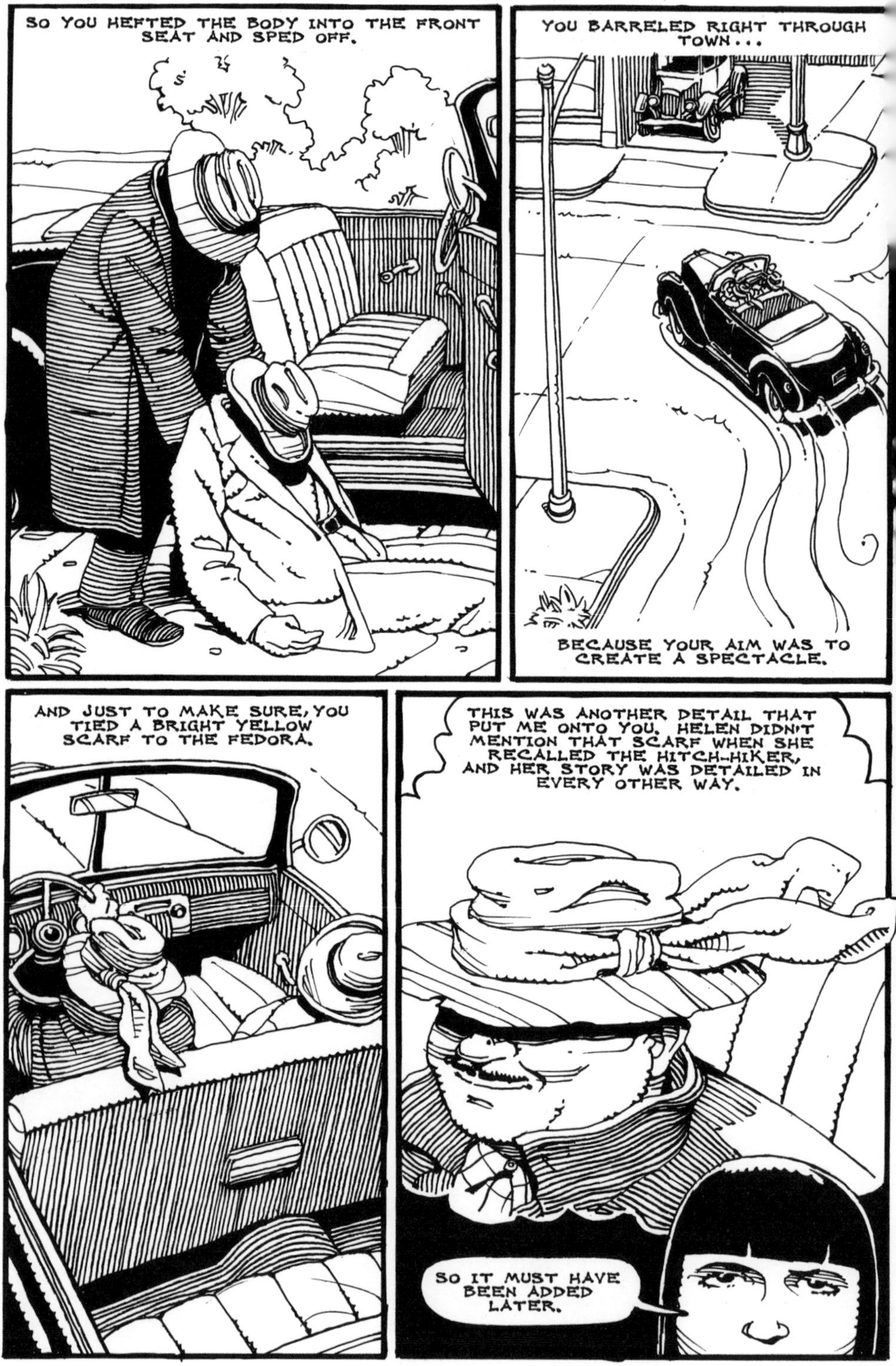
SO YOU HEFTED THE BODY INTO THE FRONT SEAT AND SPED OFF.
YOU BARRELED RIGHT THROUGH TOWN...
BECAUSE YOUR AIM WAS TO CREATE A SPECTACLE.
AND JUST TO MAKE SURE, YOU TIED A BRIGHT YELLOW SCARF TO THE FEDORA.
THIS WAS ANOTHER DETAIL THAT PUT ME ONTO YOU. HELEN DIDN'T MENTION THAT SCARF WHEN SHE RECALLED THE HITCH-HIKER, AND HER STORY WAS DETAILED IN EVERY OTHER WAY.
SO IT MUST HAVE BEEN ADDED LATER.

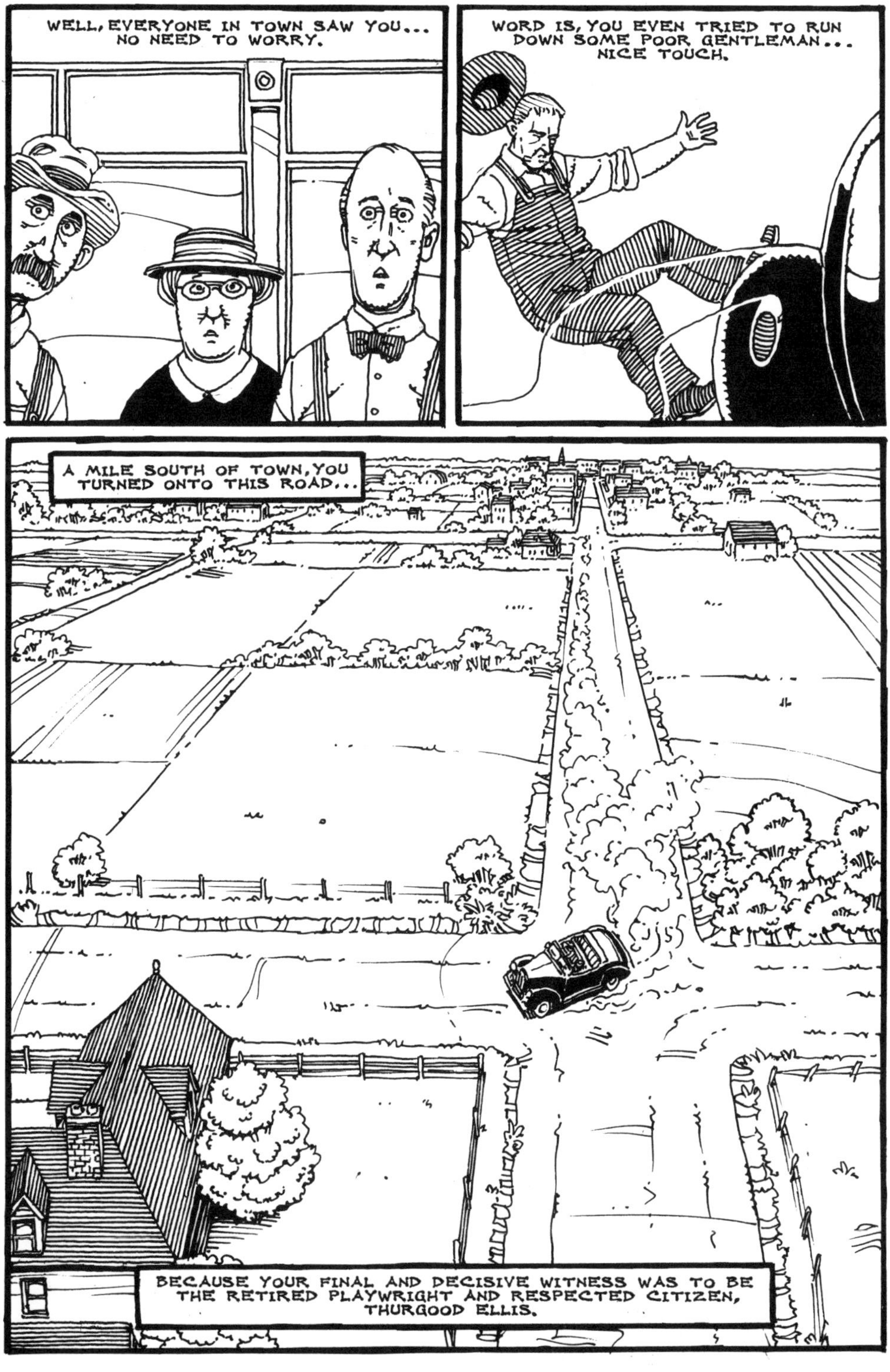
WELL, EVERYONE IN TOWN SAW YOU... NO NEED TO WORRY.
WORD IS, YOU EVEN TRIED TO RUN DOWN SOME POOR GENTLEMAN... NICE TOUCH.
A MILE SOUTH OF TOWN, YOU TURNED ONTO THIS ROAD...
BECAUSE YOUR FINAL AND DECISIVE WITNESS WAS TO BE THE RETIRED PLAYWRIGHT AND RESPECTED CITIZEN, THURGOOD ELLIS.

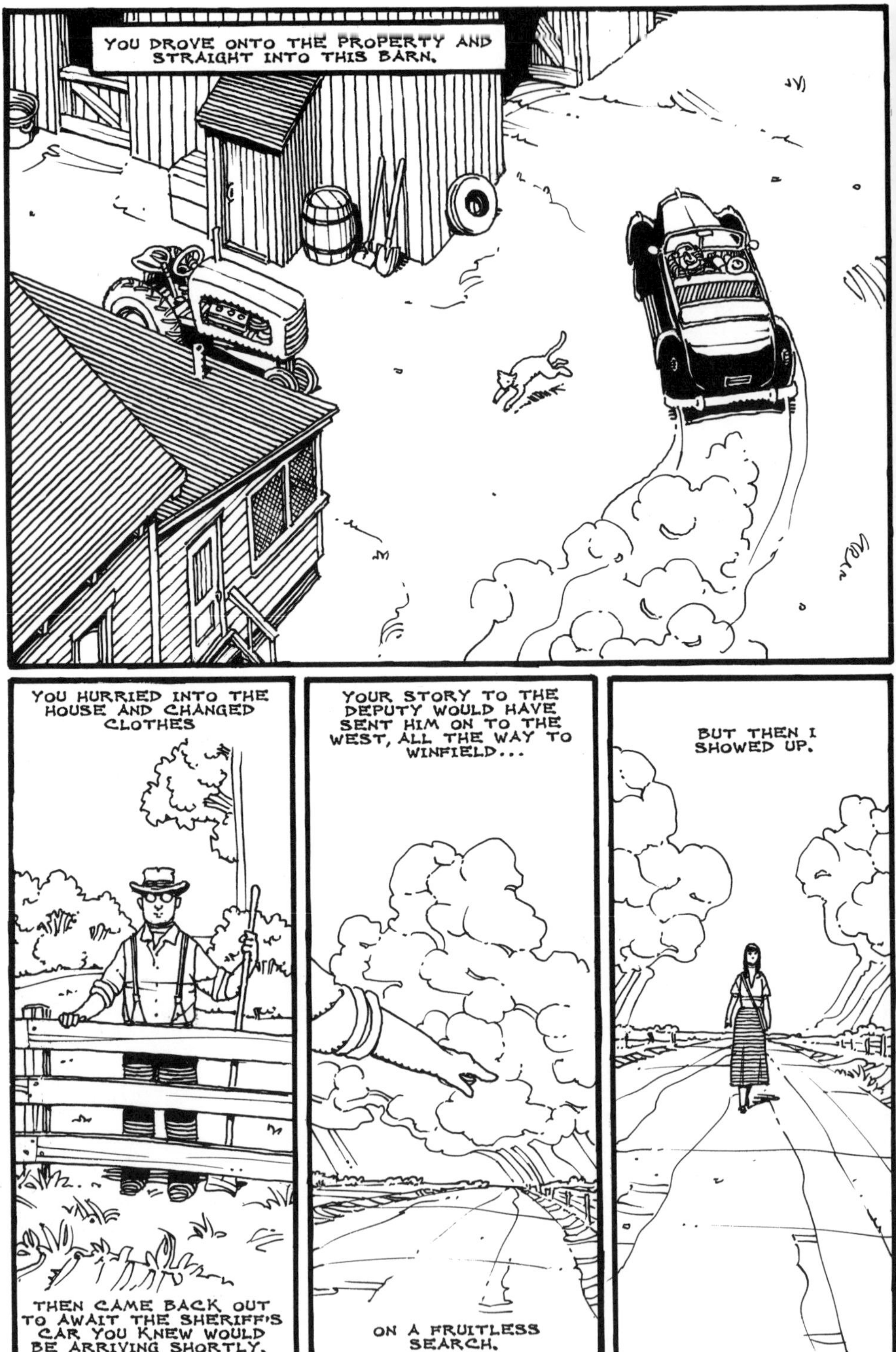

YOU DROVE ONTO THE PROPERTY AND STRAIGHT INTO THIS BARN.
YOU HURRIED INTO THE HOUSE AND CHANGED CLOTHES
THEN CAME BACK OUT TO AWAIT THE SHERIFF'S CAR YOU KNEW WOULD BE ARRIVING SHORTLY.
YOUR STORY TO THE DEPUTY WOULD HAVE SENT HIM ON TO THE WEST, ALL THE WAY TO WINFIELD...
ON A FRUITLESS SEARCH.
BUT THEN I SHOWED UP.

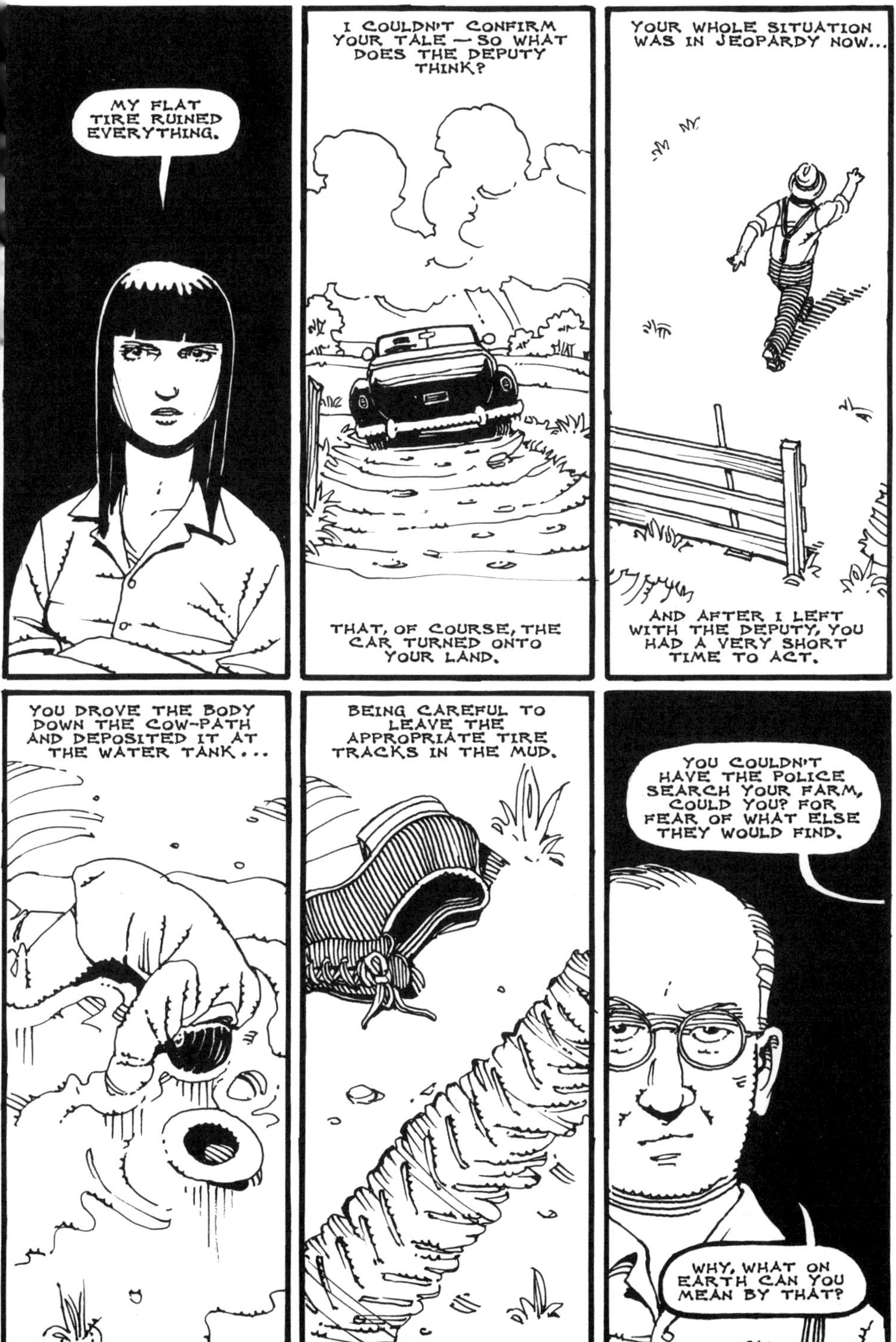
MY FLAT TIRE RUINED EVERYTHING.
I COULDN'T CONFIRM YOUR TALE — SO WHAT DOES THE DEPUTY THINK?
THAT, OF COURSE, THE CAR TURNED ONTO YOUR LAND.
YOUR WHOLE SITUATION WAS IN JEOPARDY NOW...
AND AFTER I LEFT WITH THE DEPUTY, YOU HAD A VERY SHORT TIME TO ACT.
YOU DROVE THE BODY DOWN THE COW-PATH AND DEPOSITED IT AT THE WATER TANK...
BEING CAREFUL TO LEAVE THE APPROPRIATE TIRE TRACKS IN THE MUD.
YOU COULDN'T HAVE THE POLICE SEARCH YOUR FARM, COULD YOU? FOR FEAR OF WHAT ELSE THEY WOULD FIND.
WHY, WHAT ON EARTH CAN YOU MEAN BY THAT?

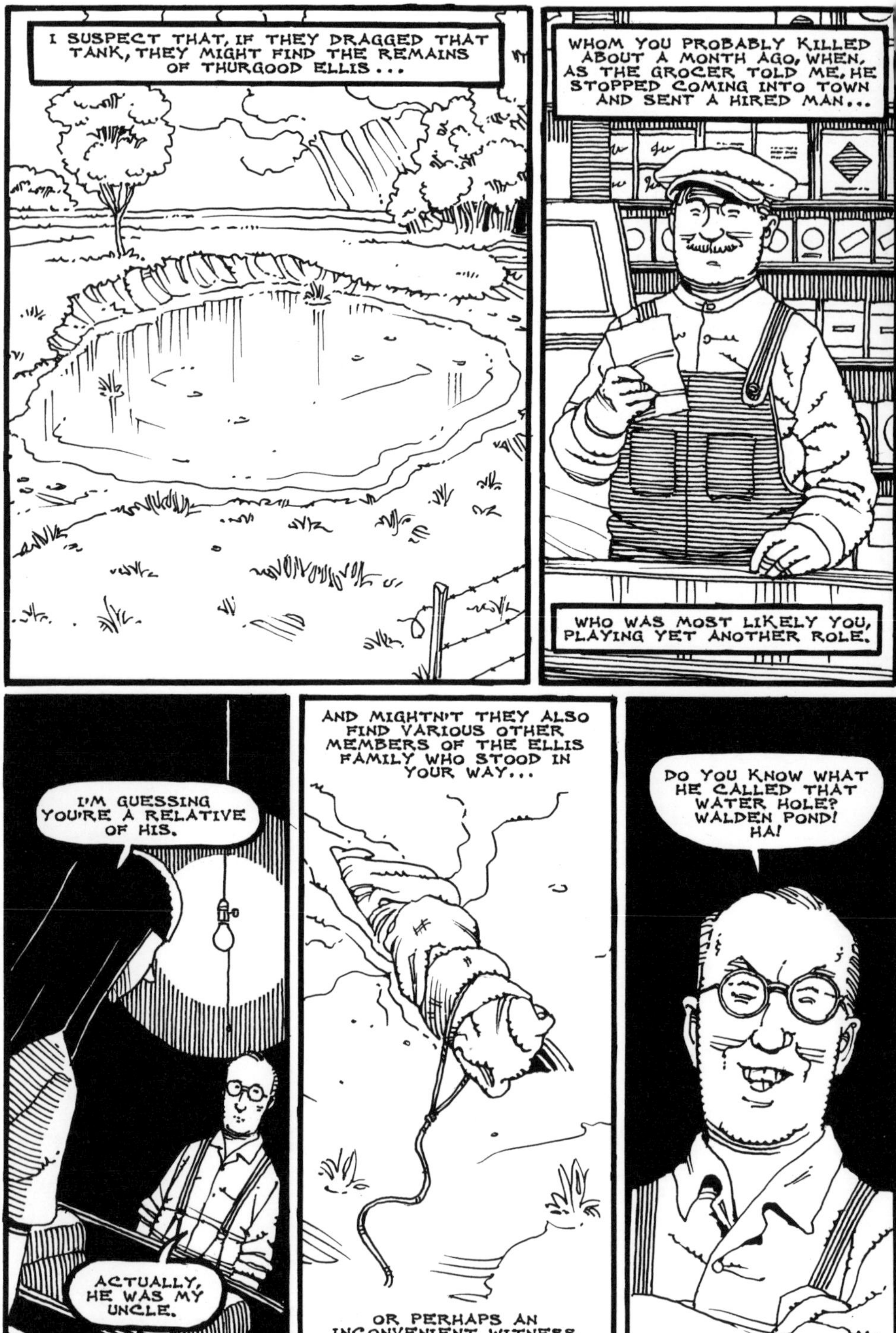
I SUSPECT THAT, IF THEY DRAGGED THAT TANK, THEY MIGHT FIND THE REMAINS OF THURGOOD ELLIS...
WHOM YOU PROBABLY KILLED ABOUT A MONTH AGO, WHEN, AS THE GROCER TOLD ME, HE STOPPED COMING INTO TOWN AND SENT A HIRED MAN...
WHO WAS MOST LIKELY YOU, PLAYING YET ANOTHER ROLE.
I'M GUESSING YOU'RE A RELATIVE OF HIS.
ACTUALLY, HE WAS MY UNCLE.
AND MIGHTN'T THEY ALSO FIND VARIOUS OTHER MEMBERS OF THE ELLIS FAMILY WHO STOOD IN YOUR WAY...
OR PERHAPS AN INCONVENIENT WITNESS OR TWO?
DO YOU KNOW WHAT HE CALLED THAT WATER HOLE? WALDEN POND! HA!

I KNEW THAT, AS I KEPT ON TALKING, I WAS PROBABLY DIGGING MY OWN GRAVE, BUT I PLOWED AHEAD ANYWAY.

ABOUT 15 YEARS AGO, I WROTE A LETTER TO THURGOOD ELLIS AND RECEIVED ONE IN REPLY.

I WENT HOME TONIGHT AND DUG IT OUT.

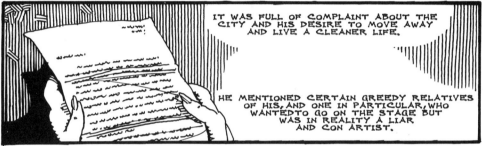

IT WAS FULL OF COMPLAINT ABOUT THE CITY AND HIS DESIRE TO MOVE AWAY AND LIVE A CLEANER LIFE.

HE MENTIONED CERTAIN GREEDY RELATIVES OF HIS, AND ONE IN PARTICULAR, WHO WANTED TO GO ON THE STAGE BUT WAS IN REALITY A LIAR AND CON ARTIST.

FLATTERING OF HIM TO SINGLE ME OUT.

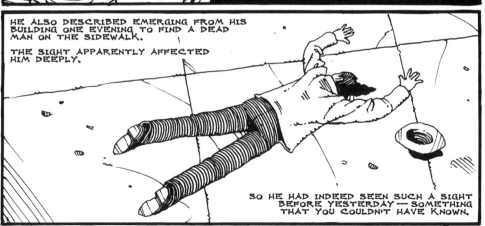

HE ALSO DESCRIBED EMERGING FROM HIS BUILDING ONE EVENING TO FIND A DEAD MAN ON THE SIDEWALK.

THE SIGHT APPARENTLY AFFECTED HIM DEEPLY.

SO HE HAD INDEED SEEN SUCH A SIGHT BEFORE YESTERDAY — SOMETHING THAT YOU COULDN'T HAVE KNOWN.

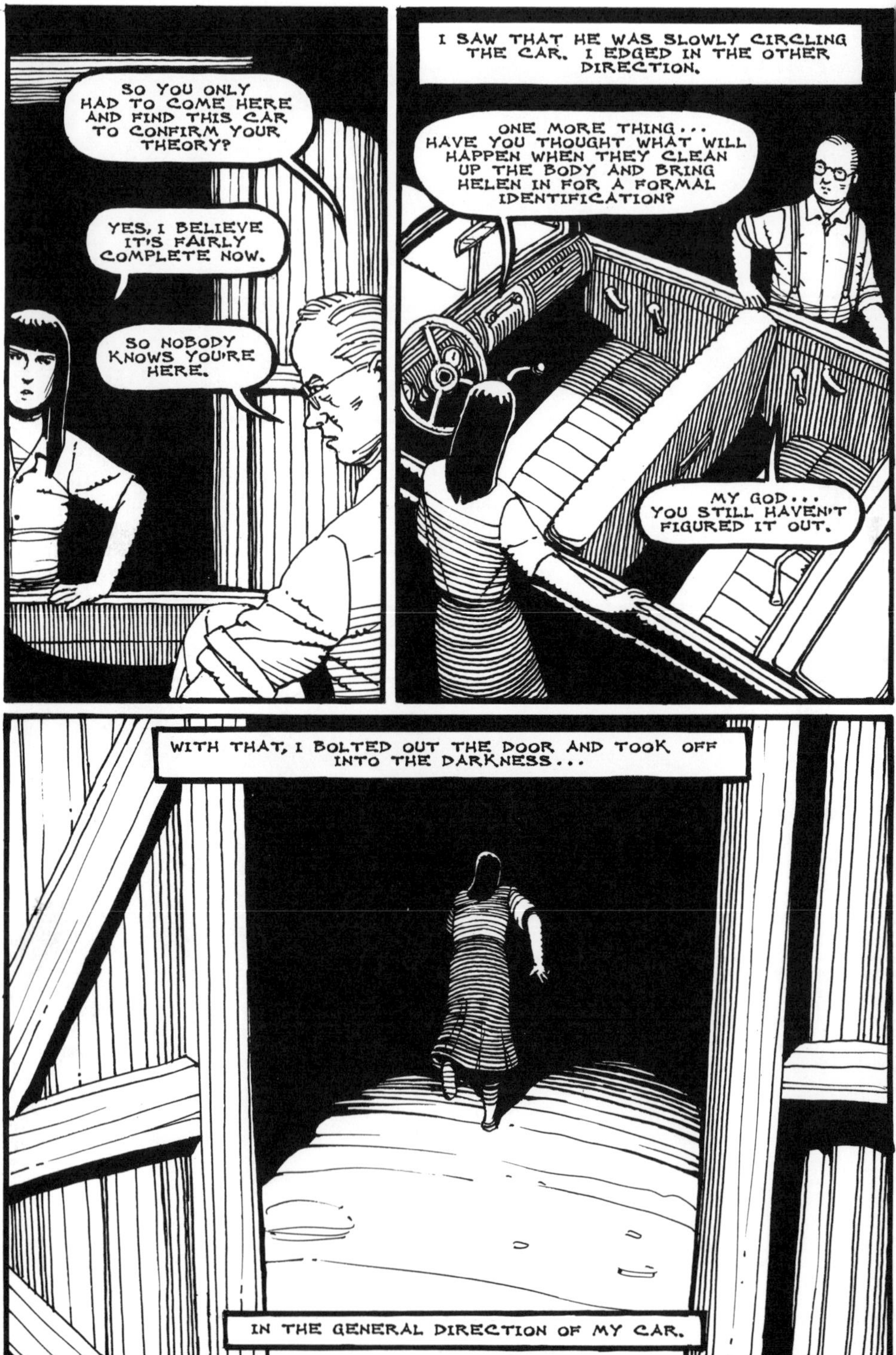
SO YOU ONLY HAD TO COME HERE AND FIND THIS CAR TO CONFIRM YOUR THEORY?
YES, I BELIEVE IT'S FAIRLY COMPLETE NOW.
SO NOBODY KNOWS YOU'RE HERE.
I SAW THAT HE WAS SLOWLY CIRCLING THE CAR. I EDGED IN THE OTHER DIRECTION.
ONE MORE THING... HAVE YOU THOUGHT WHAT WILL HAPPEN WHEN THEY CLEAN UP THE BODY AND BRING HELEN IN FOR A FORMAL IDENTIFICATION?
MY GOD... YOU STILL HAVEN'T FIGURED IT OUT.
WITH THAT, I BOLTED OUT THE DOOR AND TOOK OFF INTO THE DARKNESS...
IN THE GENERAL DIRECTION OF MY CAR.

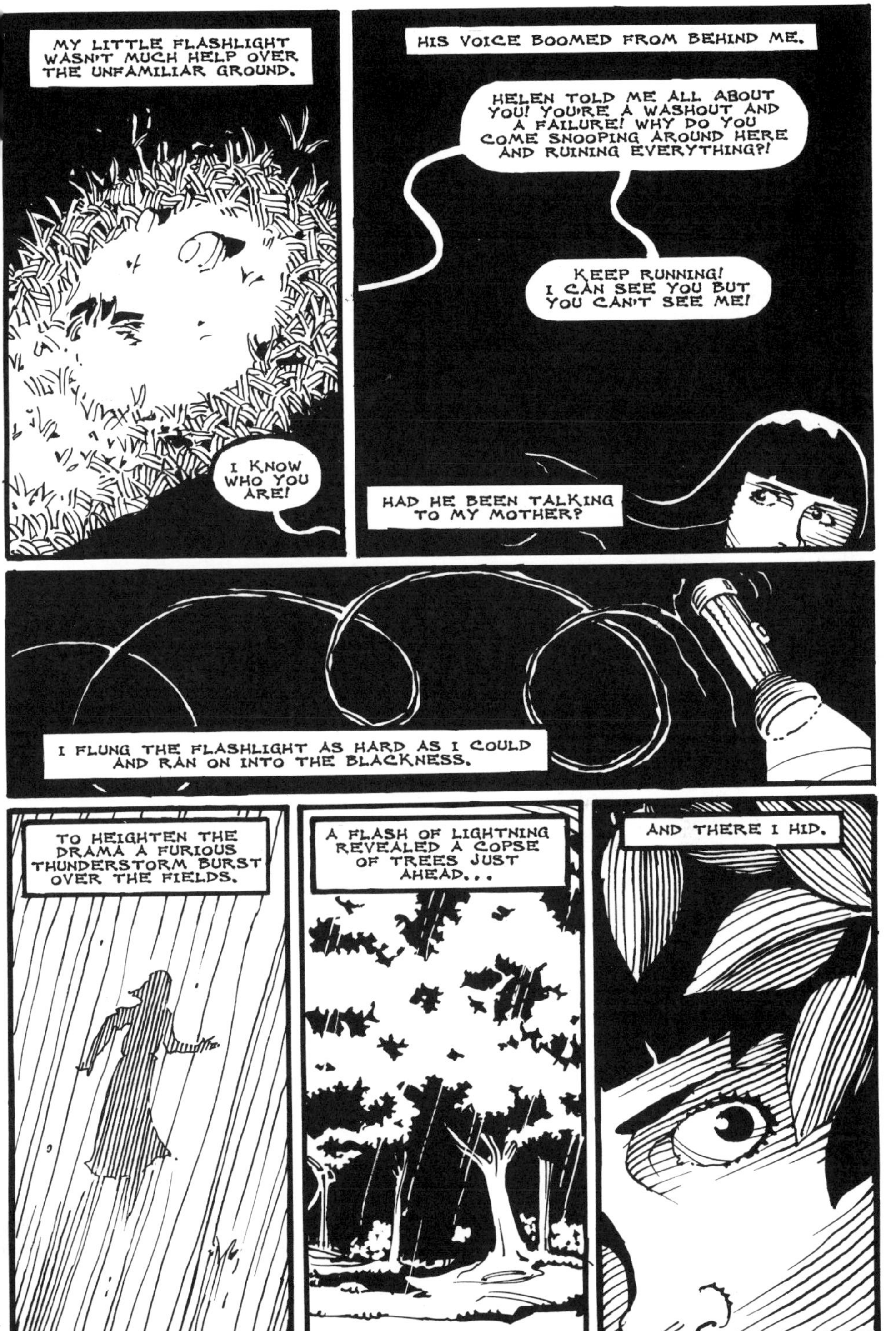

MY LITTLE FLASHLIGHT WASN'T MUCH HELP OVER THE UNFAMILIAR GROUND.
I KNOW WHO YOU ARE!
HIS VOICE BOOMED FROM BEHIND ME.
HELEN TOLD ME ALL ABOUT YOU! YOU'RE A WASHOUT AND A FAILURE! WHY DO YOU COME SNOOPING AROUND HERE AND RUINING EVERYTHING?!
KEEP RUNNING! I CAN SEE YOU BUT YOU CAN'T SEE ME!
HAD HE BEEN TALKING TO MY MOTHER?
I FLUNG THE FLASHLIGHT AS HARD AS I COULD AND RAN ON INTO THE BLACKNESS.
TO HEIGHTEN THE DRAMA A FURIOUS THUNDERSTORM BURST OVER THE FIELDS.
A FLASH OF LIGHTNING REVEALED A COPSE OF TREES JUST AHEAD...
AND THERE I HID.

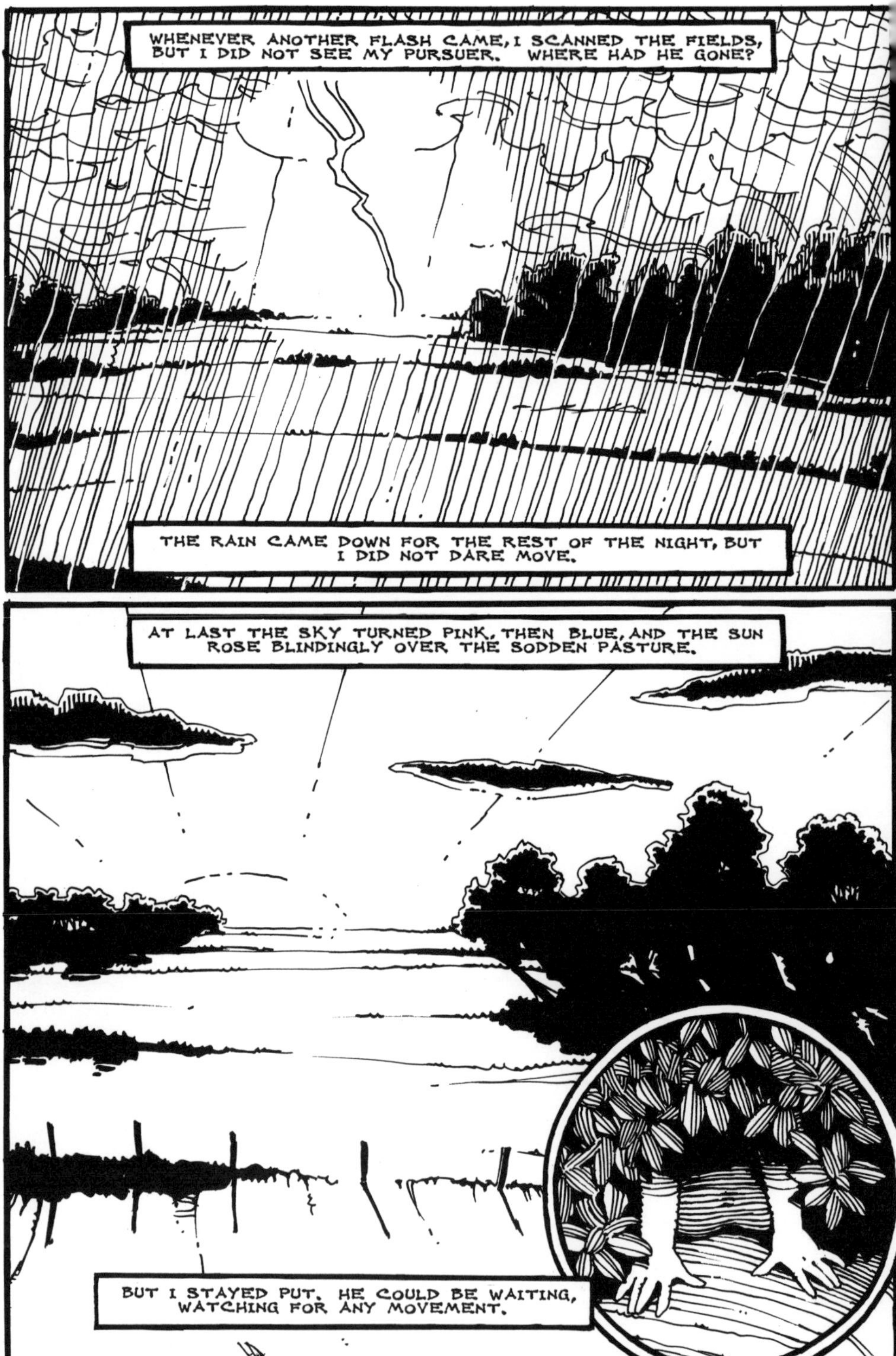
WHENEVER ANOTHER FLASH CAME, I SCANNED THE FIELDS, BUT I DID NOT SEE MY PURSUER. WHERE HAD HE GONE?
THE RAIN CAME DOWN FOR THE REST OF THE NIGHT, BUT I DID NOT DARE MOVE.
AT LAST THE SKY TURNED PINK, THEN BLUE, AND THE SUN ROSE BLINDINGLY OVER THE SODDEN PASTURE.
BUT I STAYED PUT. HE COULD BE WAITING, WATCHING FOR ANY MOVEMENT.

ABOUT MID-MORNING, I FELT SAFE ENOUGH TO TRY AND MAKE IT BACK TO THE CAR.

I MOVED SLOWLY, HUGGING THE TREE LINE.

AS I WALKED, I SCANNED THE LANDSCAPE.

THERE'S THE WATER TANK.

THEN I SAW IT: HALF SUBMERGED ON THE BANK ...

A PATHETIC END LIKE THAT OF SO MANY OF HIS VICTIMS.

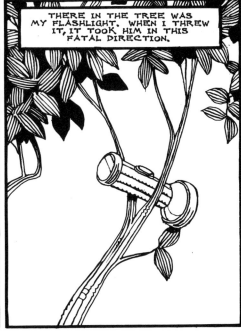

THERE IN THE TREE WAS MY FLASHLIGHT. WHEN I THREW IT, IT TOOK HIM IN THIS FATAL DIRECTION.

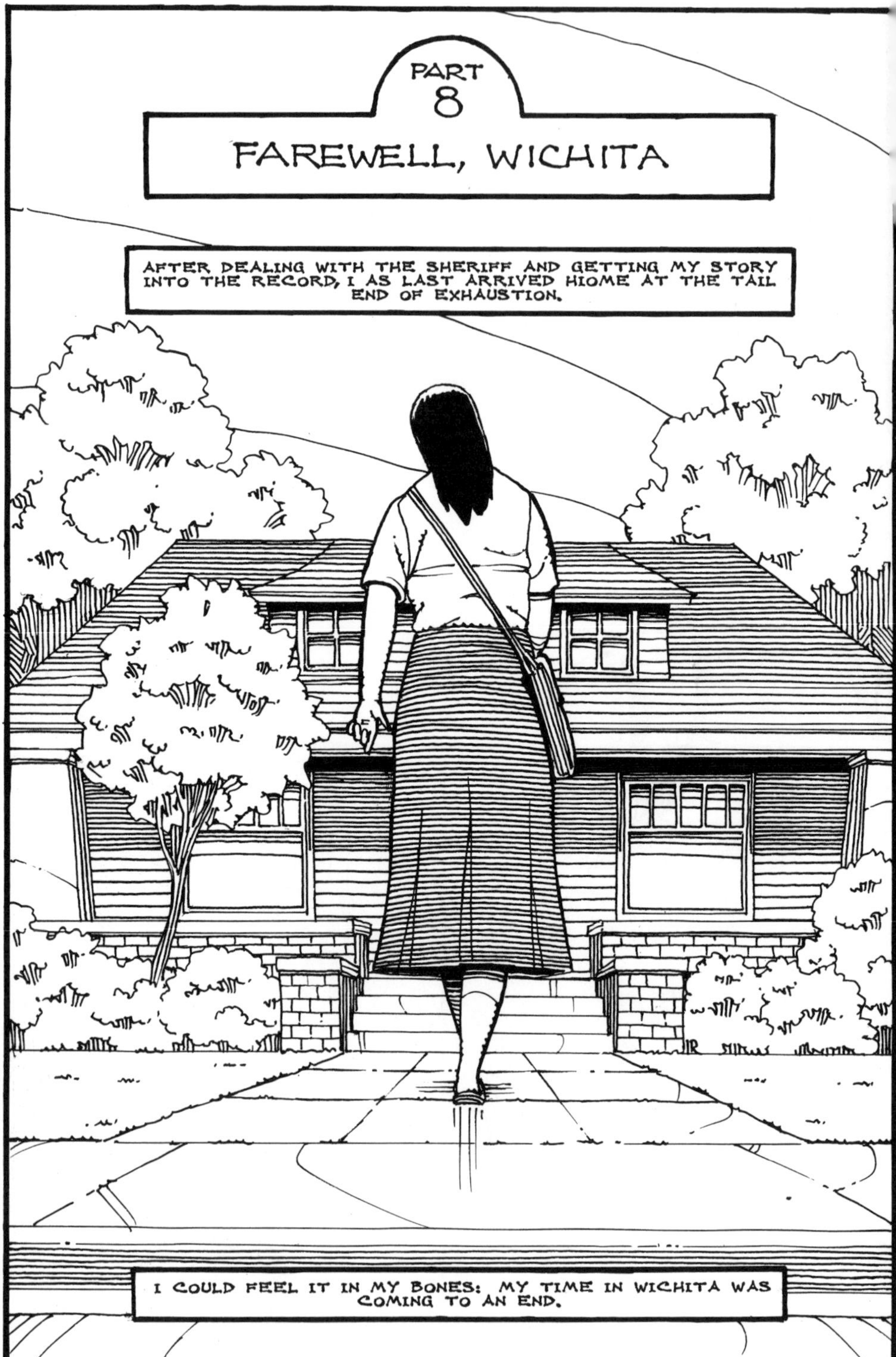
PART 8
FAREWELL, WICHITA
AFTER DEALING WITH THE SHERIFF AND GETTING MY STORY INTO THE RECORD, I AS LAST ARRIVED HIOME AT THE TAIL END OF EXHAUSTION.
I COULD FEEL IT IN MY BONES: MY TIME IN WICHITA WAS COMING TO AN END.

THE NEXT DAY, AS IF THROUGH TELEPATHY, A LETTER ARRIVED.

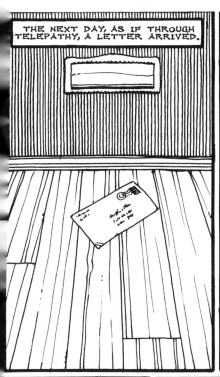

IT WAS FROM AN OLDER GENTLEMAN, AN ADMIRER WHOM I HAD KNOWN FOR YEARS.

HE INVITED ME TO NEW YORK AND OFFERED MONETARY SUPPORT UNTIL I COULD FIND EMPLOYMENT (NO STRINGS ATTACHED OF COURSE).

I HAVE TO SAY I DIDN'T HESITATE. I QUIT MY JOB AT GARFIELD'S AND BOUGHT A RAIL TICKET.

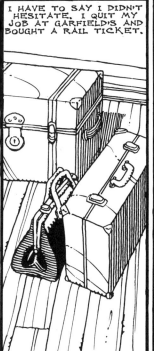

FOR THE FEW DAYS BEFORE MY DEPARTURE, I MOVED BACK INTO MY PARENTS' HOME.

DURING THAT TIME, WE WERE AGAIN A JOLLY FAMILY — MOST LIKELY BECAUSE THEY WERE RELIEVED TO SEE ME GO.

DID YOU HEAR THE NEWS?

75

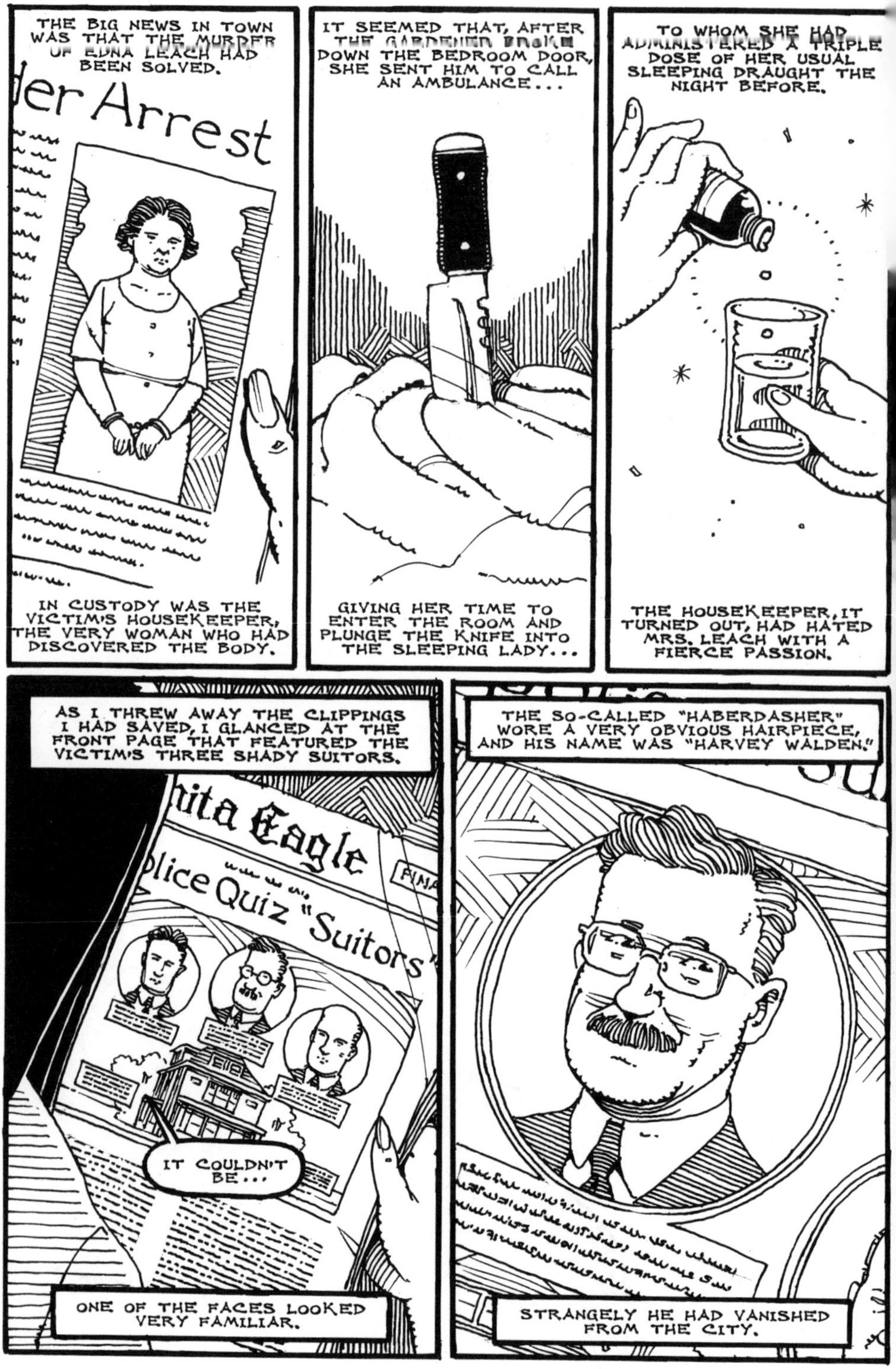
THE BIG NEWS IN TOWN WAS THAT THE MURDER OF EDNA LEACH HAD BEEN SOLVED.
der Arrest
IN CUSTODY WAS THE VICTIM'S HOUSEKEEPER, THE VERY WOMAN WHO HAD DISCOVERED THE BODY.
IT SEEMED THAT, AFTER THE GARDENER BROKE DOWN THE BEDROOM DOOR, SHE SENT HIM TO CALL AN AMBULANCE...
GIVING HER TIME TO ENTER THE ROOM AND PLUNGE THE KNIFE INTO THE SLEEPING LADY...
TO WHOM SHE HAD ADMINISTERED A TRIPLE DOSE OF HER USUAL SLEEPING DRAUGHT THE NIGHT BEFORE.
THE HOUSEKEEPER, IT TURNED OUT, HAD HATED MRS. LEACH WITH A FIERCE PASSION.
AS I THREW AWAY THE CLIPPINGS I HAD SAVED, I GLANCED AT THE FRONT PAGE THAT FEATURED THE VICTIM'S THREE SHADY SUITORS.
hita Eagle
FINA
lice Quiz "Suitors"
IT COULDN'T BE...
ONE OF THE FACES LOOKED VERY FAMILIAR.
THE SO-CALLED "HABERDASHER" WORE A VERY OBVIOUS HAIRPIECE, AND HIS NAME WAS "HARVEY WALDEN."
STRANGELY HE HAD VANISHED FROM THE CITY.

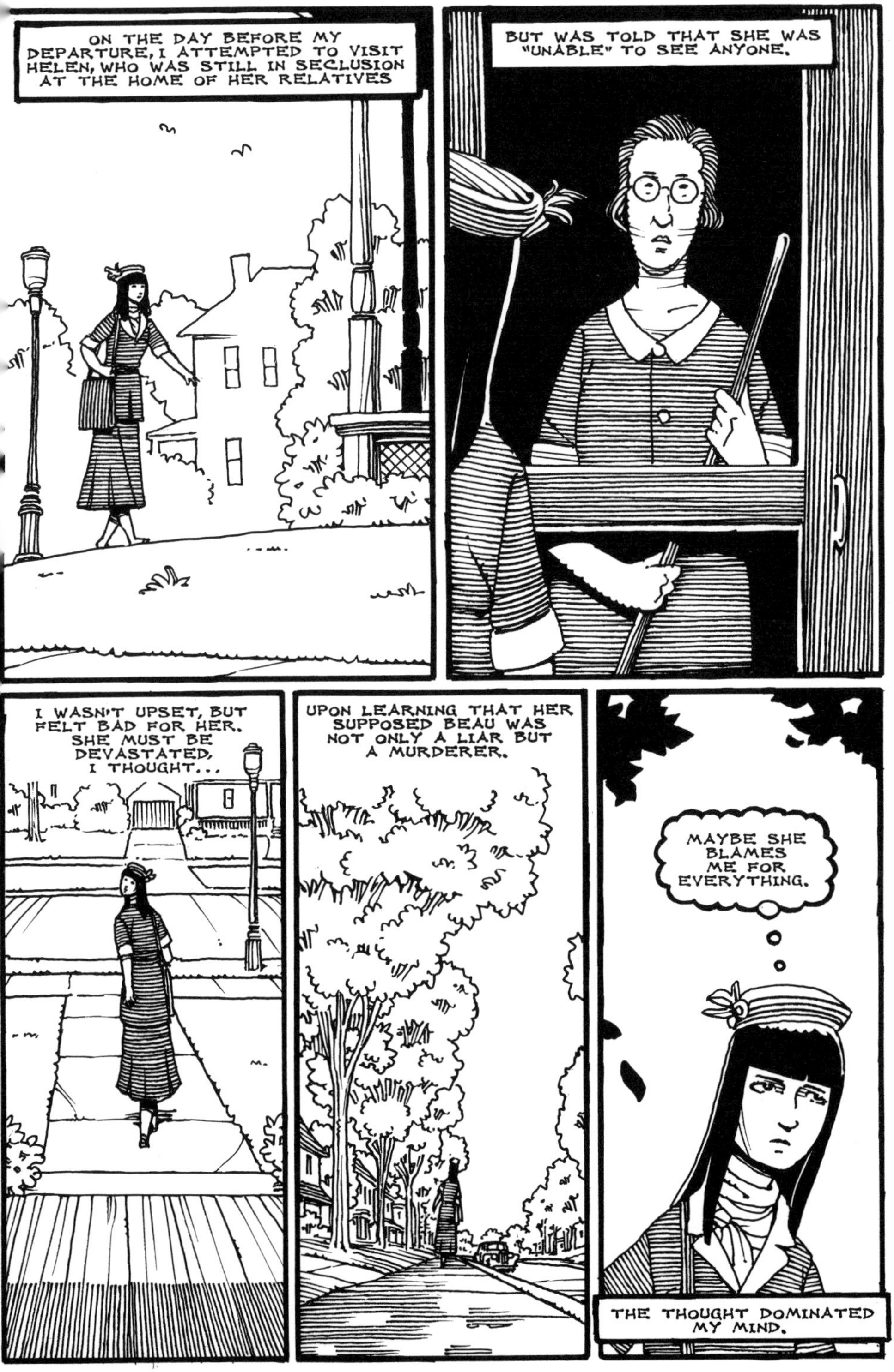
ON THE DAY BEFORE MY DEPARTURE, I ATTEMPTED TO VISIT HELEN, WHO WAS STILL IN SECLUSION AT THE HOME OF HER RELATIVES
BUT WAS TOLD THAT SHE WAS "UNABLE" TO SEE ANYONE.
I WASN'T UPSET, BUT FELT BAD FOR HER. SHE MUST BE DEVASTATED, I THOUGHT...
UPON LEARNING THAT HER SUPPOSED BEAU WAS NOT ONLY A LIAR BUT A MURDERER.
MAYBE SHE BLAMES ME FOR EVERYTHING.
THE THOUGHT DOMINATED MY MIND.

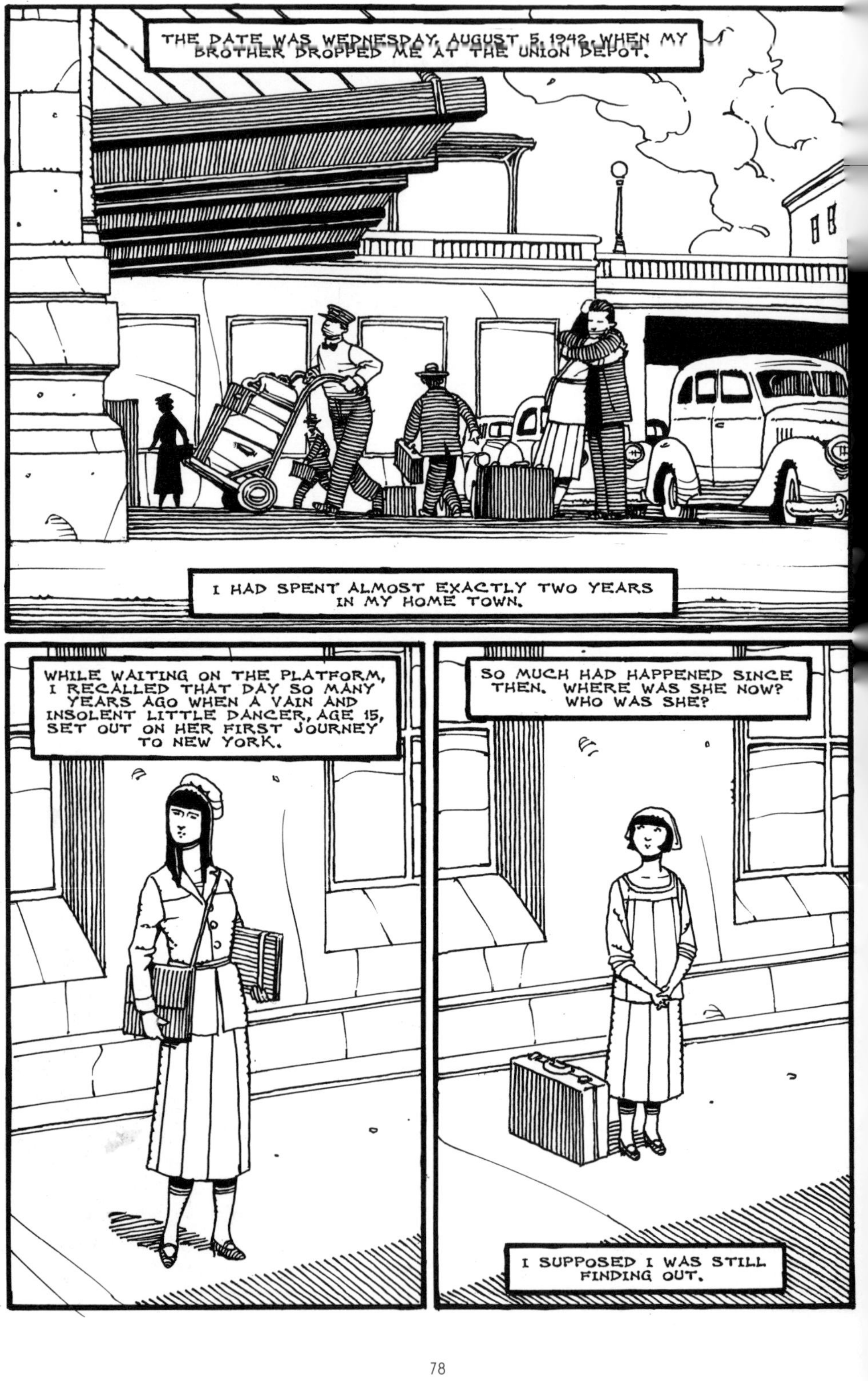
THE DATE WAS WEDNESDAY, AUGUST 5, 1942, WHEN MY BROTHER DROPPED ME AT THE UNION DEPOT.
I HAD SPENT ALMOST EXACTLY TWO YEARS IN MY HOME TOWN.
WHILE WAITING ON THE PLATFORM, I RECALLED THAT DAY SO MANY YEARS AGO WHEN A VAIN AND INSOLENT LITTLE DANCER, AGE 15, SET OUT ON HER FIRST JOURNEY TO NEW YORK.
SO MUCH HAD HAPPENED SINCE THEN. WHERE WAS SHE NOW? WHO WAS SHE?
I SUPPOSED I WAS STILL FINDING OUT.

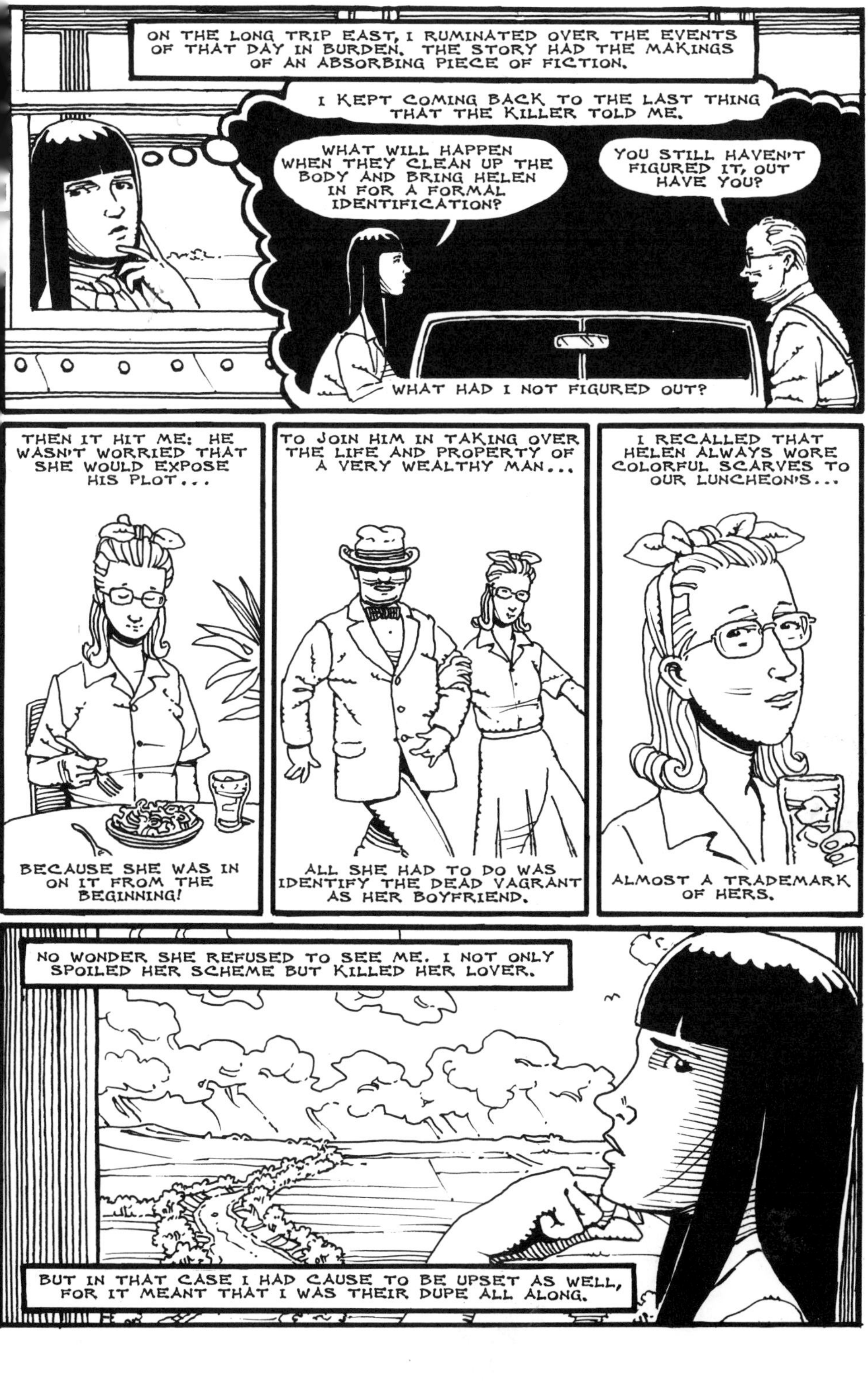
ON THE LONG TRIP EAST, I RUMINATED OVER THE EVENTS OF THAT DAY IN BURDEN. THE STORY HAD THE MAKINGS OF AN ABSORBING PIECE OF FICTION.
I KEPT COMING BACK TO THE LAST THING THAT THE KILLER TOLD ME.
WHAT WILL HAPPEN WHEN THEY CLEAN UP THE BODY AND BRING HELEN IN FOR A FORMAL IDENTIFICATION?
YOU STILL HAVEN'T FIGURED IT, OUT HAVE YOU?
WHAT HAD I NOT FIGURED OUT?
THEN IT HIT ME: HE WASN'T WORRIED THAT SHE WOULD EXPOSE HIS PLOT...
BECAUSE SHE WAS IN ON IT FROM THE BEGINNING!
TO JOIN HIM IN TAKING OVER THE LIFE AND PROPERTY OF A VERY WEALTHY MAN...
ALL SHE HAD TO DO WAS IDENTIFY THE DEAD VAGRANT AS HER BOYFRIEND.
I RECALLED THAT HELEN ALWAYS WORE COLORFUL SCARVES TO OUR LUNCHEON'S...
ALMOST A TRADEMARK OF HERS.
NO WONDER SHE REFUSED TO SEE ME. I NOT ONLY SPOILED HER SCHEME BUT KILLED HER LOVER.
BUT IN THAT CASE I HAD CAUSE TO BE UPSET AS WELL, FOR IT MEANT THAT I WAS THEIR DUPE ALL ALONG.

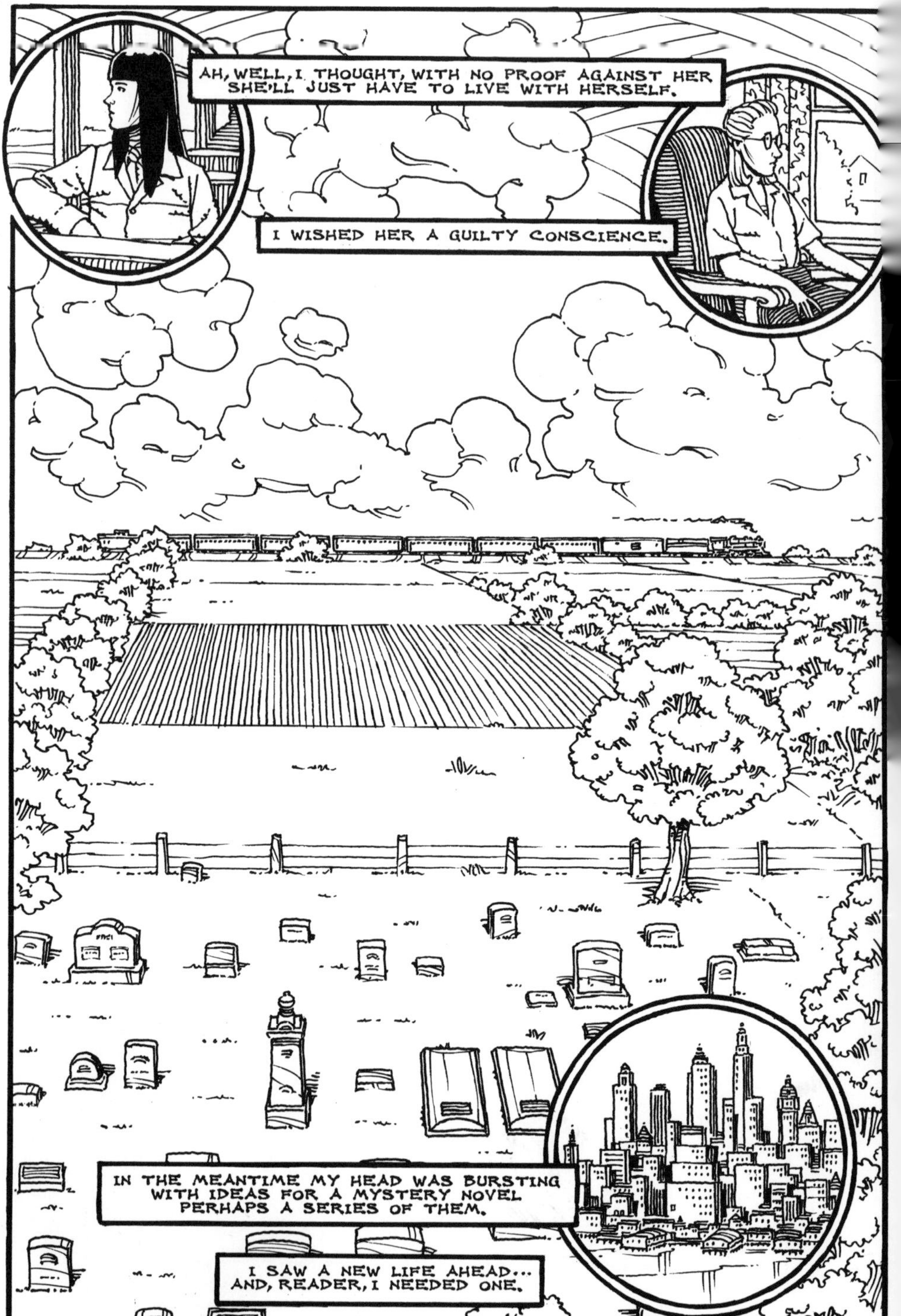
AH, WELL, I THOUGHT, WITH NO PROOF AGAINST HER SHE'LL JUST HAVE TO LIVE WITH HERSELF.
I WISHED HER A GUILTY CONSCIENCE.
IN THE MEANTIME MY HEAD WAS BURSTING WITH IDEAS FOR A MYSTERY NOVEL PERHAPS A SERIES OF THEM.
I SAW A NEW LIFE AHEAD... AND, READER, I NEEDED ONE.